LIVES

OF THE

CHIEF FATHERS OF NEW ENGLAND.

The Lord our God be with us, as he was with our fathers: let him not leave us, nor forsake us.

1 Kings 8: 57.

VOL. V.

THE LIVES

OF

INCREASE MATHER

AND

SIR WILLIAM PHIPPS.

BY ENOCH POND.

LIBRARY EDITION, 100 COPIES.

BOSTON:
1870.

PREFACE.

The first settlers of New England were remarkable men. They were raised up in Providence, for an important purpose; were trained for it by a most extraordinary discipline; and bravely, nobly, did they accomplish their vocation. Their characters, on every account, are worthy of our study. The knowledge and the benefits of their example cannot be too widely extended. I was glad, therefore, when I saw it announced, more than a year ago, that the lives of some of the chief fathers of New England were to be published, in a series of volumes, by the Massachusetts Sabbath School Society. The volumes already published have been well received, and I only regret that the one herewith presented to the public, is so little worthy to have a place among them.

Increase Mather was not a literal Pilgrim, but the son of a Pilgrim. He was born in this country soon after its settlement, and here he spent almost the whole of his long and useful life. For more than sixty years together, he was literally a *public man.* He sustained the most important offices, both sacred and civil; was called to act in the most trying and responsible situations, and although we claim for him no exemption from the infirmities incident to fallen human nature, yet it may be safely said, that to no one of her sons is New England, on the whole, more deeply indebted. A brief sketch of the life of Increase Mather, was given in a volume, entitled, "The Mather Family," published in 1843. The present Memoir, though containing some part of the former, is yet a very different work. It presents a much more full and particular account of the venerable Mather, being extended to not less than four times the same number of pages.

The first chapter of the present Memoir is chiefly occupied with biographical notices of Mr. Mather's father and brothers. My reasons for devoting so much space to them are, in brief, as follows:

In a series of volumes purporting to contain "The Lives of the Chief Fathers of New England;" it seemed quite indispensable that some account should be given of Richard Mather; and I knew not where a notice of him could be so well inserted, as here.

Then the life of Increase Mather is so intimately connected with that of his father and brothers, that, in order to a right understanding of the former, the reader needs, and *must have*, some acquaintance with the latter.

It is to be considered, too, that the Mather family was a remarkable one, more especially in its first generations;—one which exerted a controlling influence on both the civil and religious affairs of New England; and it seemed proper to preface the Memoir of the more distinguished member of it with a short introduction to the family in general. At the same time, it is hoped that the notices inserted are not without some interest in themselves, and will not be unprofitable to those who read them.

The second Memoir in the volume is that of the first *Provincial* Governor, Sir William Phipps. He was cotemporary with Increase Mather, though a little younger; and the two were associated in some of the more important transactions of their lives. It is fitting, therefore, that their Memoirs should stand together.

Sir William Phipps was in the strictest sense, what is sometimes called a *self-made man*. He commenced life under the most forbidding circumstances, and rose by his own exertions to the possession, not only of a large estate, but of the highest honors to which, in this country, he could at that time aspire. And yet he died at the early age of forty-four. The study of such a life and example cannot but be useful, more especially to the young. It will not be without interest, I hope to all.

In conclusion, I would humbly commit the volume to God, and under him to the Sabbath School Libraries, earnestly hoping that it may contribute to make known the deeds of our worthy ancestors, and to extend and perpetuate the benefits of their example.

ENOCH POND.

Bangor, April, 1847.

LIFE OF INCREASE MATHER.

CHAPTER I.

His Lineage and Family. Brief sketches of the lives of his father, Rev. Richard Mather, and of his brothers, the Rev. Messrs. Samuel, Nathaniel, and Eleazer Mather.

It was a star which guided the wise men of the East to the birthplace of the infant Saviour. In all ages there have been stars, to lead men to Christ. Such, preëminently, are learned, pious, devoted, evangelical ministers. They are burning and shining lights while here below, and having accomplished their work, and turned many to righteousness, they go to shine as stars in the firmament of heaven forever.

Among the stars in the right hand of the great Head of the Church, which glittered upon the golden candlesticks, of primitive New England, none shone with a brighter and more attractive lustre, than Increase Mather. I propose, in what follows, to make my readers acquainted with this venerable man;—but in order to do it to the best advantage, it will be necessary to premise a brief account of his *lineage*, and *family*.

He was the son of Rev. Richard Mather, long the faithful and successful minister of Dorchester, Mass. Richard Mather was born in the small town of Lowton, Lancashire, England, A. D. 1596. He was early sent to a public school at Winwick, where he was boarded in the winter; but in the summer, (so great was his desire for learning,) he walked daily four miles to school, from his father's house. He suffered much, while at school, from the unreasonable strictness and severity of his teacher,—so much that he often entreated his father to take him away, and permit him to relinquish his studies altogether. But to this his father would not consent, but encouraged him to persevere; and for his firmness in this instance, the world is under lasting obligations to the good man; and Mr. Mather himself did not cease to remember him with gratitude and honor, as long as he lived. "God intended better for me," he said, "than I would have chosen for myself; and therefore my father, though in other things indulgent enough, yet in this would never condescend to my request, but by putting me in hope that, by his speaking to the master, things would be amended, would still over-rule me to go on in my studies. And good it was to me to be overruled by him and his discretion, rather than to be left to my own affections and desires."

Let children learn, from this example, to confide in their parents' judgment, rather than in their own. Many an individual besides Richard Mather, has found and acknowledged in after life, the benefit of having been crossed in his childish wishes, and of having been compelled to pursue a course of life very different from that which he would himself have chosen.

It is evidence of the proficiency of young Mather, and of the confidence which his too rigid master reposed in him, that he recommended him as teacher of a public school at Torteth Park, near Liverpool, when he was only fifteen years of age. He continued in this school several years, discharging the duties of preceptor, with distinguished success, and perfecting himself, meanwhile, in those branches of study which he had occasion to teach. It was while he was here, that he became a subject of renewing grace. The principal means of his awakening was that best of all preaching—the strict and holy *example* of the Christian with whom he boarded. "The exemplary walk of this godly man," whose name was Aspinwall, "caused many sad fears to arise in his own soul, that he was himself out of the way; which consideration, with his hearing a Mr. Harrison preach about regeneration, and his reading Mr. Perkins' book, showing *how far a reprobate may go in religion*, were the means whereby the God of heaven brought him into the state of the *new creature*. The troubles of soul which preceded his new birth were so exceedingly terrible, that he would often retire from his meals into secret places, to lament his miseries. But after some time, the good Spirit of God healed his broken heart, and poured into it the consolations of his great and precious promises."

From this period, Mr. Mather seems to have had his mind fixed upon the holy ministry; and that he might prepare himself in the best manner, for so great a work, he resolved to relinquish his school, and connect himself with the University at Oxford. His residence at Oxford could not have been more than two or three years; for in 1618, when he was only twenty-two years of age, he received an invitation to return to Torteth, not as a schoolmaster, but as a minister of righteousness.

He was ordained, together with several others,

by Dr. Morton, bishop of Chester. When the ordination was over, the bishop took him aside, and addressed him in the following remarkable language: "I have an earnest request unto you, Mr. Mather, and you must not deny me. It is that *you would pray for me.* I know that the prayers of such as fear God, will avail much, and I take you to be of this number."

In 1624, two years after his settlement at Torteth, Mr. Mather was married to an excellent lady, the daughter of Edmund Holt, Esq., of Bury, who was his assistant in labor, and the partner of his pilgrimage, for more than thirty years.

During his ministry in England, Mr. Mather was abundant in labors, not only among his own people, but in the adjoining towns and villages. He always seized the opportunity which his attendance at funerals afforded, for imparting instruction to the living. He frequently preached upon holidays; because, as he says, "there was then an opportunity to cast the net of the gospel among a multitude of fishes." Great assemblies were then brought together, which otherwise would have been worse employed.

Having spent about fifteen years in the diligent and faithful performance of duties such as these, complaints were at length urged against him for non-conformity; and in August, 1633, he was suspended from the ministry. By the intercession of friends, his suspension was removed after a few months; but it was again inflicted the next year, and under circumstances which led him to despair of being ever more permitted to exercise his ministry in his native land.

About this time, Mr. Mather entered renewedly, and more thoroughly than ever before, upon the study of church polity, assisted by the writings of such men as Cartwright, Parker, Baines, and Ames. The result was, that he became a decided Congregationalist, and was henceforth known as the expounder and earnest defender of Congregational principles.

By the opening of the year 1635, Mr. Mather had made up his mind to join the goodly number of confessors and pilgrims, who were bidding adieu to their native land, and migrating to the distant shores of New England. The reasons which satisfied him as to the propriety of this important measure, were the following, as recorded by himself: "It is right to remove,

1. From a corrupt church to a purer.

2. From a place, where the truth and the professors of it are persecuted, unto a place of more quiet and safety.

3. From a place where all the ordinances of God cannot be enjoyed, unto a place where they may.

4. From a church, where the discipline of the Lord Jesus Christ is wanting, unto a church where it may be practiced.

5. From a place, where the ministers of God are unjustly inhibited from the execution of their functions, to a place where they may more freely execute them.

6. From a place, where there are fearful signs of coming desolations, to a place where one may have a well-grounded hope of God's protection."

Such were the reasons which led to Mr. Mather's removal from England to America; and such, for substance, were the reasons which influenced *all* the pilgrims. Here is nothing said about gold and silver, about commercial enterprises and gains; but every one of the six reasons has respect to *religion*,—its purity, the liberty of professing and practicing it, and the anticipated favor of God in the undertaking. These reasons are enough, of themselves, to show the nature of the enterprise in which our fathers were engaged. It was primarily and chiefly a *religious* enterprise,—undertaken for the enjoyment and advancement of religion, and the glory of God. And in the success of it, we have a remarkable illustration of that declaration of the Psalmist: "Surely the wrath of man shall praise thee." During the twelve years of Archbishop Laud's administration, not less than four thousand emigrants became planters in America. Neale, informs us, that he had a list of seventy-seven divines, ordained in the church of England, who became pastors of churches in America, before the year 1640.

Among these divines was the Rev. Richard Mather. Fleeing in disguise from his persecutors, who were in hot pursuit of him, he embarked at Bristol, in May, 1635, and arrived with his family at Boston, in August of the same year. Near the end of the voyage, he encountered a terrible storm at sea, and was on the point of being swallowed up, but the Lord graciously preserved him, to be an ornament and blessing to the infant churches of New England.

Before his arrival, the church which had been first planted at Dorchester, under the charge of Rev. Mr. Warham, had removed in a body, with its pastor, and settled at Windsor, Connecticut; leaving the remaining settlers at Dorchester, in a destitute state. Mr. Mather was almost immediately called to exercise his ministry among them, and after due consultation, he consented to become their pastor, and here he continued to the day of his death, a period of more than thirty-three years. After the downfall of the hierarchy, he was earnestly solicited to return to his former charge in England; but he rightly judged that the Lord had called him to this country, and that it was his duty here to spend his days.

The preaching of Mr. Mather is represented as being not only sound, and instructive, but very direct and plain. He "studiously avoided obscure and foreign words, and the needless citation of Latin sentences, aiming to shoot his arrows, not over the heads, but *into the hearts* of his hearers." Yet so scripturally and powerfully did he preach his plain sermons, that Mr. Hooker used to say, "My brother Mather is a mighty man." In both Englands, he had much success of his labors in converting many souls to Christ. One of Mr. Mather's hearers, speaking of events which took place in Dorchester, soon after his settlement, says: "In those days did God manifest his presence among us, in converting many souls, and in gathering his dear ones into church fellowship by solemn covenant. Our hearts were taken off from old England, and set upon heaven. The discourse, not only of the aged, but of the youth also, was, not *How shall we go to England?* but, *How shall we go to heaven? Have I true grace wrought in my heart? Have I Christ, or no?* O the many tears that were shed in Dorchester meeting-house, at such times, both by those who declared God's work on their souls, and by those that heard them!"

At the period of which we are speaking, much attention was given, both in this country and in England, to the subject of *church government.* Our fathers had little dissension or discussion about the leading *doctrines* of the gospel. These, having settled down upon the good old scriptural foundation of Calvinism, had scarcely began to be disputed. The *doctrinal* articles of the several reformed churches were remarkably at agreement. But many points of church government and discipline were still undecided. The sense of the inspired writers in regard to them had not been satisfactorily ascertained. It was with reference to these, undoubtedly, that the famous John Robinson expected more light to break forth from the Scriptures, and exhorted his people to follow that light.

To these points, therefore, the minds of our forefathers and their cotemporaries were directed, with a deeply interested attention; and it is evidence of the high standing of Mr. Mather among them, and of the estimation in which he was held, that his services were in continual requisition, in resolving and defending points of this nature. In the year 1639, thirty-two questions, relating to church government, were propounded by the general court of Massachusetts, for the consideration of the ministers. Their answer to these questions was drawn up entirely by Mr. Mather. He was a prominent member of the synod of 1648, and with his own hand drew up the substance of the celebrated Cambridge Platform, which was then adopted. He is said to have been a member of every synod that was convened in New England, during his residence in the country; and was actually the moderator of an ecclesiastical council, at the time of his death. This circumstance led one of his brethren to write for him the following memorial: " *Vixerat in Synodis; moritur moderator in illis;*—Among Synods he lived; the moderator of one he died.

He was one of three ministers, who prepared the New England version of the Psalms;—a work more creditable to his piety and orthodoxy, than to his poetical inspiration. He wrote an answer to Mr. Davenport of New Haven on the subject of infant baptism,* with which old Mr. Higginson, of Salem, was so well pleased, that he said: "Mr. Mather is a pattern to all the answerers in the world." He was the author of several other works, chiefly (though not wholly) on his favorite subject of church order and discipline.

Mr. Mather was not only an active, but an eminently *studious* man. "So intent was he upon his beloved studies, that only the morning before his death, he importuned the friends who were with him to help him into his study," where he had not been for several days, and where, he remarked, "My usual works and my books expect me. Is it not lamentable that I should lose so much time?"

Up to the period of his last sickness, the health of Mr. Mather had been uninterruptedly good. He had never been obliged to call a physician; had never been sick of any acute disease, nor in fifty years together had he been detained so much as one Lord's day from his public labors. His last illness was that distressing one, the stone, with which he was attacked while attending an ecclesiastical council in

* The question between them did not respect the *validity* of infant baptism, but the lawfulness of baptizing any except the children of church members, in full communion.

Boston. He was able to be removed to his own house, but never to leave it afterwards. In the paroxysms of his complaint, he seldom groaned, but was a pattern of patience to all around him. He fortified his soul under suffering, by reading Dr. Goodwin's Discourse upon Patience, which he continued to do to the day of his death. When inquired of as to his health, his usual answer was, *Far from well; yet far better than mine iniquities deserve.* He died in peace, April 22, 1669, aged seventy-three, having been for more than fifty years a preacher of righteousness.

It is remarkable that the last sermon which Mr. Mather preached to his people, being then in usual health, was from these words: "I am now ready to be offered, and the time of my departure is at hand. I have fought a good fight; I have finished my course; I have kept the faith: Henceforth there is laid up for me a crown of righteousness, which the Lord, the righteous Judge shall give me at that day." 2 Tim. 4: 6—8. The sermon before the last was from these words: "All the day of my appointed time will I wait, till my change come." Job. 14: 14. A sermon which he had not preached, but which was prepared just before his last fatal attack, was from these words: "We know that if our earthly house of this tabernacle were dissolved, we have a building of God, a house not made with hands, eternal in the heavens." 2 Cor. 5: 1. It has long been a favorite opinion with some, that holy men have not unfrequently a presage of their approaching dissolution, before the event actually overtakes them. How far the facts above stated may go to confirm such an opinion, I leave for my readers to decide.

About twenty years previous to his death, Mr. Mather was called to part with the wife of his youth, and the mother of his children;—a most excellent help-meet, "by whose discreet management of his affairs, he had been so released from all secular incumbrances, as to be wholly at liberty for the sacred employments of the ministry." She died with the following words on her lips: "Eye hath not seen, nor ear heard, neither have entered into the heart of man, the things which God hath prepared for them that love him."

Mr. Mather was united in a second marriage with the widow of his distinguished ministerial brother, the Rev. John Cotton, of Boston. This lady survived him. By his first marriage, he had six sons, four of whom graduated at Harvard College, and were able and faithful ministers of Christ.

The eldest of the sons, Samuel Mather, was born in England, and was brought by his father to this country, when about nine years of age. He became hopefully pious in mere childhood, and is represented as an extraordinary instance, not only of early developed intellectual ability, but of "discretion, seriousness, prayerfulness, and watchfulness." The Arabians have a tradition that when John Baptist was a child, the other boys asked him to play with them. But he refused, saying, '*I was not sent into the world for sport.*' Such seem to have been the thoughts of the child, Samuel Mather, so far as his thoughts were indicated by his general course of life.

He graduated at Harvard College in the year 1643, at the early age of seventeen, and was the first of the graduates who was detained there, in the capacity of tutor. While at Cambridge, he enjoyed the instructive and powerful ministry of Rev. Thomas Shepard;—a privilege which he greatly prized, and for which, after the decease of Mr. Shepard, he felt himself called upon to make some compensation, by publishing a Memoir of him to the world. In proof of the estimation in which Mr. Mather was held as a tutor, it is stated, that when he read his last lecture in the College hall, nearly all the students were in tears; and that when he took his leave of the college, they actually put on badges of mourning.

At the formation of the second or North Church in Boston, Mr. Mather was applied to, to be their minister. He preached to them their first sermon, and continued with them through the winter following; but having a strong desire to visit England, which was his native land, he went thither in the year 1650.

As the hierarchy was now prostrate, there was nothing in the way of his advancement in England, where his popularity as a preacher was even greater than it had been in his own country. Almost immediately on his arrival, he was appointed chaplain to the lord mayor of London, in which situation he became early acquainted with some of the most eminent ministers in the land. During his residence in London, he was so often called upon to preach, that his health was seriously impaired, and he was thought to be in danger of losing his life. After a respite, however, his accustomed vigor was restored; and we next hear of his preaching at Gravesend; and then at the cathedral in the city of Exeter. After this, he was appointed

Chaplain of Magdalen College, Oxford, where he remained for a considerable time. From this situation, in which he seems to have been both useful and happy, he was called to accompany the English commissioners on their tour into Scotland, where he continued his labors for about two years.

In 1660, in connection with Dr. Harrison, Dr. Winter, and Mr. Charnock, he went with the lord deputy, Henry Cromwell, into Ireland. He was here appointed senior fellow of Trinity College, Dublin, and joint pastor with Dr. Winter of the church of St. Nicholas. An opportunity was here presented for the exercise of that true Christian liberality, for which Mr. Mather was ever distinguished; for when the lord deputy gave him a commission for the displacing of several Episcopal ministers, he refused to do it, saying, "I came into this country to preach the gospel, not to hinder others from preaching it."

This was a measure of liberality, however, which was not meted to him again; for almost immediately upon the restoration of Charles II., he was himself suspended on a charge of sedition. This charge—a spiteful and malicious one—was founded on two discourses which he had preached in opposition to the Episcopal rites and ceremonies, and especially to the enforcing of them by the rigors of the law. When Mr. Mather was notified of his suspension, and of the groundless charge on which it was based, he said: "If it be sedition to disturb the devil's kingdom, who rules by his antichristian ceremonies, in the kingdom of darkness, as the Lord Jesus does by his own ordinances in his church, I may say that *I did it*, before the Lord, who hath chosen me to be his minister; and if this be vile, *I will yet be more vile.*"

When Mr. Mather could no longer exercise his ministry in Ireland, he returned to England, and established himself at Burton Wood, Lancashire, where he continued about two years; until, with two thousand of his faithful brethren, he was ejected by the terrible act of uniformity, in 1662.

Being denied the privilege of preaching in England, except on conditions with which he could not in conscience comply; Mr. Mather now returned to his friends in Dublin, where he founded a Congregational Church, and set up a meeting in his own hired house. And here he continued, without further molestation, to the day of his death.

The Mr. Mather of which we now speak, like

several of the other members of his family, accomplished much as an author. He had occasion to go repeatedly into the Popish controversy, and write in defence of the Protestant religion. He preached and published against what he conceived to be the errors of the established church, while he was ever disposed to treat godly ministers and members of that church with affection and respect. He published a work, entitled *Irenicum*, the design of which was to promote a greater degree of union and harmony among the three principal denominations of English Dissenters, the Presbyterians, Congregationalists, and Baptists. This was an object on which his heart was much set, and to further which he did not labor altogether in vain. He wrote also on the prophecies of Scripture; and a volume of sermons on the types.

He had a controversy with an individual in Dublin, on a subject not altogether unlike some of the marvels of our own times. There was a man there who affirmed that he had the gift of healing diseases, by stroking and rubbing the diseased parts with his hands. Thousands flocked to him from all parts of Ireland; some noblemen, some learned and pious persons, and even ministers of the gospel. Mr. Mather had no faith in the impudent quack, and prepared a discourse with a view to expose him. This fell into the hands of some of the king's privy council in Ireland, by whom it was highly approved and applauded.

Mr. Mather was an example of fidelity, in all the relative and social duties. To his honored father whom he had left in this country, he was in the habit of sending valuable donations, year by year, as long as he lived. Of his younger brothers he was also mindful, and assisted materially in preparing them for usefulness. In the year 1656, he was married to a sister of Sir John Stevens, by whom he had several children, only one of whom survived him. His wife died in 1668, when they had lived together about twelve years. Her closing scene was uncommonly peaceful. While in her last agonies, her husband said to her, "You are just going where there will be no more pain." "Ah, yes," she replied, "and what is better, where there will be no sin." When her sister said to her, "You are going to heaven," she answered, "I seem to be there already, Come, Lord Jesus, come quickly."

Mr. Mather survived his companion only about three years. He died in Dublin, Oct. 29, 1671, at the early age of forty-six, and was buried in the church of St. Nicholas, of which he had formerly been the pastor. The following epitaph was written for him, but whether actually inscribed on his tombstone, it does not appear: "*Diu vixit, licet non diu fuit.*" He *lived* long, although he did not *continue* long.

As a preacher, Mr. Samuel Mather stood in the first rank. His name was known throughout the three kingdoms. His discourses were remarkable for clearness of reason, and method, and for the majesty and authority with which they were uttered. It used to be said by critics of those times: "Mr. Charnock's invention; Dr. Harrison's expression; and Mr. Mather's logic, would make the perfectest preacher in the world."

The second of the sons of Richard Mather, of which we have any account, was the Rev. Nathaniel Mather. He was born in England, and came with his parents to this country when he was five years old. Like his brother Samuel he graduated at Harvard College at the age of seventeen. After he had entered the ministry, he followed his brother into England, and was presented by the Protector Cromwell to a living in Barnstable, in 1656. Here he continued until 1662, when, with his brother, he had the honor to be one of that noble band of two thousand, who were ejected for non-conformity.

Scarcely anything has occurred in the whole history of Christianity, more truly honorable to religion, than the conduct of these ejected ministers, on this occasion. In the first place, there was a vast body of them, including the ablest and best men in the kingdom. Then they were in quiet possession of comfortable livings, and these, in most instances, constituted their whole living. They were surrounded with families, wives and children, whose earthly prospects and comforts all depended on their retaining their places. They were themselves dependent on their professional labors for a subsistence, the most of them not having been trained to any other employment, nor knowing how to obtain a livelihood in any other way. And then all that was required of them was to stretch their consciences, more or less, so as to submit to the Episcopal rites and forms, and give their countenance to what they conceived to be superstitious and unwarrantable additions in the public worship of God. And yet, *their consciences could not be stretched.* They knew how to make sacrifices, to embrace poverty, to endure hardships and privations, to go (if it must be) to prison and to death; but to play the hypocrite—to trifle with conscience—to do what they verily believed would be displeasing to God, merely for the sake of gaining their bread,—they had no heart. They preferred to take the spoiling of their goods, to retire from their livings, to renounce at once their earthly all, and to cast themselves, naked and dependent, but yet believing and confident, upon the grace and providence of their heavenly Father. Verily, here is evidence that there was some conscience still remaining in England, and that the revival of religion, which preceded and followed the overthrow of Laud's tyrannical administration, had not been altogether without fruit.

The firmness of this noble band of confessors will appear in a stronger light, if contrasted with what took place in England, a little more than a century afterwards. In the year 1772, about two hundred and fifty clergymen of the church of England, who were Unitarians, petitioned Parliament, that they might be relieved from subscribing to the articles of the church, on the ground that such subscription was against their consciences. But the House of Commons, rejected their petition, and the subscription was enforced, as usual. And now what did these distressed Unitarian churchmen do? With the exception of a single individual, (Mr. Lindsey,) they clung to their livings, and to the emolu- ments of a church whose doctrines they had publicly declared they did not believe; and Mr. Lindsey was left to complain, that of the multitudes in the establishment who concurred in his sentiments, only *one* was found willing to contribute towards the expense of erecting him a chapel.

But to return to Mr. Mather. Being no longer at liberty to preach in England, he passed over to Holland, and became pastor of an English congregation at Rotterdam. Here he remained until the death of his brother Samuel, when he was invited to take the charge of his bereaved and afflicted church at Dublin. He was afterwards pastor of a Congregational church in London, and one of the lecturers at Pinner's Hall. He died July 26, 1697, and was interred in the burying ground near Bunhill Fields. On his tombstone, the traveler may still read a long Latin inscription, prepared by Dr. Watts, which ascribes to him a high character for genius, learning, piety, and ministerial fidelity.

He was the author of several works, the principal of which are, a treatise entitled, "The Righteousness of God by Faith, upon all who Believe;" and a little volume of sermons preached at Pinner's Hall. The sermons were taken down in short hand, as they were delivered, and published after his death.

The memorials of the Rev. Nathaniel Mather have chiefly perished. We have not the means of forming a judgment respecting him, as we have in the case of his father and brothers. But from the several important stations which he occupied, the circles of piety in which he moved, the works which he published, and especially from the character given of him by Dr. Watts, there can be no doubt that he was a learned, gifted, devoted and faithful minister of the Lord Jesus Christ. It was his lot to live in a trying period—an era of storm, revolution, and conflict; but he bore the test, he kept the faith, and has gone to receive the crown of righteousness, which the Lord, the righteous Judge, shall give him at that day.

The third of the sons of the Rev. Richard Mather, who went into the ministry, was named Eleazer. He was born in Dorchester, May 13, 1637, and graduated at Harvard College in 1656. He immediately commenced preaching, being at the time but nineteen years of age. He did not follow the example of his brothers, and seek a field of labor in the cities of the old world, but rather preferred the rude settlements of the new. He was the first minister of Northampton, Massachusetts. Having preached to the people about two years, a church was gathered, and he was ordained its pastor, June 23, 1658. He died July 24, 1669, the same year with his venerable father, and when he had been settled only eleven years. He is represented as a "very zealous preacher, and pious walker," who was instrumental in bringing many souls to the Saviour. His death was greatly lamented, not only by his own church, but by all the then infant churches on the Connecticut river.

As he approached the end of life, "he grew so manifestly ripe for heaven, in a holy, watchful, fruitful disposition," that many pious persons anticipated his speedy removal. The following are the last words that he wrote in his diary; "This evening (July 10, 1669,) I had some sweet longings of soul after God in Christ, according to the terms of the covenant of grace. The general and indefinite expression of the promise was an encouragement to me to look to Christ, that he would do that for *me*, which he has promised to do for *some*. Nor do I dare exclude myself; but if the Lord will help me, I will live at his feet, and accept of grace in his own way and time, through his power enabling me. Though I am dead, and without strength, help, or hope in myself, yet the Lord requireth nothing at my hands in *my own strength*, but that, by his power, I should look to him, to work all his works in me and for me."

When the Rev. Richard Mather lay dying, one of his sons said to him: "Sir, is there any *special* thing which you would wish me to do, in case the Lord should spare me on earth, after you are in heaven?" To this the venerable man, with lifted eyes and hands, replied: "A special thing which I would commend to you is, *care concerning the rising generation in this country*, that they be early brought under the government of Christ in his church." Acting on this suggestion of his dying father, Mr. Eleazer Mather immediately commenced preaching a series of sermons for the benefit of the young. As this was the last of his public labors, so it was considered by his people as the best. These "pungent sermons" were published after his death, and widely circulated among the youth of New England.

The wife of Eleazer Mather was the daughter of the Rev. John Warham, first minister of Dorchester, and afterwards first minister of Windsor, Connecticut. After his death she was married to his successor, the celebrated Solomon Stoddard; and was grandmother of the still more celebrated metaphysician and divine, Jonathan Edwards. The only daughter of Mr. Mather was married to the Rev. John Williams of Deerfield. She was carried into captivity, and cruelly murdered by the Indians, in the winter of 1704. Deerfield was at this time a frontier town, and much exposed to the incursions of the savages. On the night of February 28th, a party of them broke into the house of Mr. Williams, murdered two of his children and a servant before his eyes, and compelled the rest of his family—himself, his wife, and surviving children—to set out immediately on their march for Canada. In wading a small river, the second day after their capture, Mrs. Williams fell down from exhaustion, and fatigue. Finding her unable to proceed further, one of the Indians despatched her with his tomahawk. Mr. Williams survived his captivity, returned to Deerfield, and continued there till his death, in 1729.

CHAPTER II.

The birth and childhood of Increase Mather. Influence of his mother. His College life. Narrative of his religious experience. He commences preaching. Visits England. His studies and labors there. Returns to New England.

THE sixth and youngest of the sons of Richard Mather, and the fourth of their number who entered the ministry, was *Increase Mather*;—the more especial subject of the present Memoir. He was born at Dorchester, June 21, 1639, and received his name, *Increase*, from the *increasing* and prosperous state of the colony, at that period. Like many other eminent ministers, he was greatly indebted, in early life, to the prayers and counsels of a pious mother. She used to say to him, while yet a child, that she desired only two things on his behalf; one was the grace to love and fear God; the other, that he might have the requisite learning and ability to accomplish something for God in the world. "My child," said she, "if God make thee a good Christian, and a good scholar, thou wilt have all that thy mother ever asked for thee." She earnestly inculcated upon him the lesson of *diligence*, and used often to repeat to him that saying of Solomon: "Seest thou a man diligent in his business; he shall stand before kings; he shall not stand before mean men."* His excellent mother died, when her son was about fifteen years of age. She exhorted him, at the last, to resolve upon serving Christ in the work of the ministry, and encouraged him to form such a resolution by saying: "They that be wise shall shine as the brightness of the firmament, and *they that turn many to righteousness as the stars forever and ever*." The impression of this scene and of this declaration, uttered under these solemn circumstances, was never effaced from the mind of her son. It had its influence in the formation of his character, and was precious to him all his days.

It is evidence of the capacity and diligence of young Mather, that he entered Harvard College when only twelve years of age. When he had been a member of College about a year, his parents, fearing that his health might suffer from the confinement and discipline of college life, removed him to the family of the celebrated

* This remark of Solomon, Increase Mather remembered and observed, and it was remarkably fulfilled upon him, as we shall see. He did literally *stand before kings*.

John Norton, then of Ipswich, afterwards of Boston. Here he remained between one and two years, pursuing college studies, and keeping up with his class.

Hitherto, though moral and amiable in his external deportment, he had made no pretensions to serious religion. He "had walked," as he expresses it, " in the vanity of his mind, was alienated from the life of God, and unmindful of the great work and end," for which he had been sent into the world. But in the year 1654, a little before his mother's death, he became the subject of a change, the fruits of which proved it to be saving and eternal. The account of it must be given in his own words.

" The great care of my godly parents was to train me up in the nurture and admonition of the Lord ; whence I was kept from many visible outbreakings of sin, which else I had been guilty of, and whence it was that I had many good impressions of the Spirit of God upon me, even from my infancy. Nevertheless, I swam quietly in the stream of impiety and carnal security, for many years together, till, in the year 1654, the Lord in mercy was pleased to visit me with a short but distressing sickness. For this happy sickness I have many a time blessed the Lord, and I trust I shall bless him forever; for it was made the means of the first saving awakenings to my soul. I was brought now to have real thoughts of death, and could see eternity before my eyes. My sins, unrepented of, also stared me in the face. After I was recovered, the arrows of God still stuck fast in my heart, and I was in much distress for months together. I now resolved that I would no more live in any known sin, and thought there was no sin in my heart from which I was not truly willing to part. I also engaged in the practice of duty, and was constant in my secret devotions, which, before these distresses of soul, I had many times neglected. Nevertheless, my wounded conscience still remained with me, and God set my sins in order before me, bringing those to my remembrance, in all their aggravations, which I had long forgotten. He showed me the vanities of my childhood, and made me to possess the iniquities of my youth, until my heart, sometimes, was ready to sink and die within me. I now resolved that I would afflict my soul with *fasting*, as well as praying, and seek more earnestly unto God for the pardon of mine iniquities. This course I took at Dorchester, shutting myself up, during my father's absence, in his study, and writing down those particular sins which pressed most heavily on my conscience, and imploring of God that he would pardon them. At this time I thought, that if the whole world were mine, I would freely part with it, to have my hard heart taken from me; and I pleaded earnestly that Divine promise which says, "I will take away from them the heart of stone, and will give them an heart of flesh." But still my flinty heart remained unmoved.

"Thus my soul continued in the new birth, and very sore were the pangs of it. Sometimes I was afraid that I had committed the unpardonable sin; but upon discourse with my father about the nature of that sin, I became satisfied that I was not guilty of it. Then I thought my sins were *too great* to be forgiven; but after reading a book of Mr. Hooker's entitled, "The Doubting soul drawn to Christ,' I saw clearly that the *greatness* of sin was no hindrance to the exercise of forgiving mercy. Being thus rid of my doubts as to the *ability* of God to save me, I was next pressed with doubts as to his *willingness* to do it; and I was foolishly ashamed to acquaint any body with my troubles, I was loth to have any one know that mine iniquities were gone over my head, as a heavy burthen too heavy for me.

"At length, when I could hold out no longer, the hand of God still pressing me sore, I acquainted my father with some of my soul distresses, stating to him in writing how it was with me, and begging him to pray for me. I resolved upon setting apart another day, to be spent in secret prayer, with fasting, before the Lord; and *a happy day this was to me! A day I shall never forget while I have a being!*

"It was the day of our anniversary election, when the scholars at Mr. Norton's were all abroad at their diversions, that I took the opportunity of a private chamber, and shutting myself up, I spent the whole day in pouring out my complaints before the Lord. Towards the close of the day, being full of distress and anguish, on account of my sin, it was put into my heart that I must go and throw myself down at the feet of my Saviour, and see whether he would accept of me, or no; resolving that if he would accept of me, then I would be his; but if not, then I would perish at his feet. So I came before him with those words of Esther, 'If I perish, I perish.' Yet I said, 'Lord, if it must be so, I am resolved to perish at the feet of thy mercy. It is true, I am a dog, and am unworthy of so much as a crumb. I have been a great sinner. Yet I am resolved, the Lord helping me, that I will not so offend any more; but I will be thine thine only, and thine forever.' And while I was thus praying and pleading, those words of Christ were darted into my mind: 'Him that cometh to me, I will in no wise cast out,' which promise I pleaded with the Lord. After that, I had some comfortable persuasion that my sins were forgiven, and that the Lord would show me mercy. And thus I went on happily, and walked with God.

"But after some time, Mr. Norton showed, that a man might forsake his sins, and have been in some sorrow of heart for them, and yet not be *truly converted.* This word stuck deep in my heart, and I was afraid that, though I had been in unspeakable sorrow for my sins, and thence had forsaken them, yet my conversion might not be sound. But hearing my father preach on these words: 'The whole have no need of a physician, but they that are sick,' I thought the sermon was preached wholly for myself. My father showed, that where there was new and true obedience, and the heart was changed from the love of sin to the love of God, it argued *conversion;* and on examination, I found *it was so with me.* My father also answered a scruple which was in my heart. I had feared my faith was not right, because it was not the preached word, but a season of *affliction*, that was the first means of my more effectual awakening. But he showed that the conversion of Manasseh was effected by the same means.

"Sometime after this, Mr. Mitchell of Cambridge preached on these words: 'Behold an Israelite *indeed*, in whom is no guile.' He pressed much to self-examination, laying down several marks of sincerity; as when God in Christ has become the rest of the soul; when there is no known sin indulged, or duty neglected; and when the heart is for God, chiefly, wholly, universally. I set myself upon a serious self-examination by these marks, and found that my heart went along with the word. So I went on cheerfully in the ways of God. And if in anything I have been overtaken in a fault, the Lord has given me to see it, and mourn for it, and turn from it."

I have transcribed this narrative at length, because I deem it one of deep and instructive interest. It is interesting to trace the germs, the beginnings of true piety, in an individual who afterwards became so distinguished. It is interesting to see the way in which a soul is led to Christ. With considerable variety, it is interesting to witness the general *uniformity* of the Spirit's operations, in such cases. First, young Mather is *awakened*, under near apprehensions of death and eternity. Then, his *sins* are set in order before his eyes. Though an outwardly moral and amiable youth, such as some would say had almost no sin, he *is distressed* in view of his sins, and the impression is constantly growing upon him, that they are *many and great.* Next, he sets himself to an outward reformation,—breaking off from every known sin, and scrupulously performing every known duty,—in hope of making some amends for the past. Still, his convictions increase upon him; and the great adversary, no longer hoping to divert or quiet him, is bent on driving him to despair. He has probably committed the unpardonable sin; or if not, his sins are too many and great to be forgiven. Or if God *can* forgive such a sinner, there is no certainty that he will. At length, despairing of help in himself, or from any other quarter, he resolves to *cast himself at the feet of Christ*, and if he must perish, he will perish there. And here he finds, what every sinner who does the same will find, *comfort and peace.* The Saviour receives him into his gracious arms, raises him up, puts a new song into his mouth, and gives him joy and peace in believing. And though, subsequently he has occasional seasons of doubt and darkness, yet his doubts one after another are dissipated, his fears subside, the light increases upon his path, and he is enabled to go on his way rejoicing. And now how many thousands are there in the church of God, who see, in all this, little more than a transcript of their own experience. They have been led substantially in the same way. They know what these convictions and distresses, these hopes, and fears, and joys mean; for they have felt the same.

Again, it is interesting to observe the manner in which God was preparing this young man for *distinguished usefulness*. Unquestionably, the best adapted instrument which God can employ for the conversion of sinners, is a *converted sinner*;—not an angel, who has never sinned, and who, of course, is not in a situation to sympathize with sinners;—not a sinner *unconverted*, who, like a finger-board at the corner of the street, can only point to a path in which he has never traveled; but a CONVERTED SINNER. Thus taught the celebrated Mr. Perkins, two hundred and fifty years ago. "It is meet that they who are to convert others, should be *effectually converted themselves*. John must first *eat the book*, and then prophesy. So ministers of the gospel must first *eat* the book of God themselves, which is truly done, when their minds are not only enlightened by it, but their hearts are mollified, and they are brought into subjection to Christ. Unless Christ be thus learned, *spiritually* and *really*, ministers will speak the word of God as men speak riddles, and as the priests in former times said their matins, when they hardly knew what they said." Such men as Paul the Apostle, and Augustine, of Hippo, and Martin Luther, and John Bunyan, and Increase Mather, and George Whitefield, could never have proclaimed the gospel as they did, and been the instruments of leading such multitudes to Christ, had they not first waded the deep waters themselves, and learned in their own experience the depth of their necessities, and the efficacy of atoning blood.

Mr. Mather, at the time of his conversion, was a member of college, whence he proceeded, at the same time with his brother Eleazer, in 1756. The next year he commenced preaching, when he could not have been more than eighteen years of age. His first sermon was preached at Dorchester, under which his venerable father was so much affected, that he could scarcely pronounce the blessing, for tears.

It will be recollected that Mr. Mather had two brothers, settled ministers in Europe; Samuel at Dublin, and Nathaniel in England. At the earnest request of his elder brother, he concluded to follow them to that field of labor.

At his departure, his aged father wept over him, and blessed him, and said: "If I hear well of you, and if you prove faithful to Christ, the joy of it will lengthen out my life." His old friend and counselor, Mr. Mitchell of Cambridge, gave him the following parting injunction: "My serious advice to you is, that you keep out of company, so far as Christianity, and civility, and occasions will give you leave. Take this from me: The time spent in your study, you will generally find spent *most profitably*, *most comfortably*, and *most accountably*." This is that Mr. Mitchell of whom Richard Baxter said: "If there could be convened an œcumenical council of the whole Christian world, that man would be worthy to be moderator of it."

Mr. Mather sailed from Boston, July 3d, 1657, and after a voyage of five weeks, was landed in England. His first year abroad was spent as a student at Trinity College, Dublin, where he took his second degree, in 1658. After leaving Ireland, he went to London, where he made the acquaintance of the celebrated John Howe, at this time one of the chaplains of the Protector Cromwell. By the advice and influence of Mr. Howe, he was introduced to a congregation at

Great Torrington, in Devonshire, where he spent the following winter, preaching the gospel to a numerous assembly, and with much acceptance.

The next spring, Mr. Mather became chaplain to the English garrison on the island of Guernsey. Here he labored to make himself useful, and observing the Lord's day to be much profaned, he preached with such power and success on the fourth commandment, that a considerable reformation was effected in the island.

We next hear of him at St. Mary's in England, preaching in the forenoon in the church, and in the afternoon at the cathedral. His feelings inclined him to settle here; but as the Protector was now dead, and Charles II. was about to be proclaimed, he saw a change of times at the door. Indeed, he publicly warned his people, from Rev. 11: 7, that further sufferings were in store for the faithful witnesses of Christ.

After a few months, he returned to his chaplaincy at Guernsey, and here he remained, till he was driven away by the rigors of conformity. He must either conform to the revived superstitions of the church of England, or leave the Island. In Dorsetshire, he had the offer of a living of four hundred pounds a year, if he would but conform, and read the common prayer; but he refused. In short, all things around him conspired to admonish him, that there was no longer a field of usefulness open for him in England, and that it was his duty to return to his native land. Wherefore, in June, 1661, he set sail from Weymouth, England, and arrived at Boston about the first of September. He came to Dorchester very unexpectedly on a Saturday evening, to the great joy of his excellent father. Here he had the happiness to meet his brother Eleazer, who had just arrived at the paternal mansion from his settlement in Northampton. "The comforted old patriarch," says Cotton Mather, "had the privilege of having his two sons in his own pulpit, on the following day, while he sat shining between them, like the sun in *Gemini*."

CHAPTER III.

Mr. Mather's marriage. His children. His settlement at Boston. His temptations. His want of pecuniary support. His diary His plan of study and of life.

Mr. Mather spent the first winter after his return to New England in preaching alternately, one Sabbath for his father in Dorchester, and the other for the new church in the North part of Boston. The following year, he was married to Maria Cotton, only daughter of the distinguished John Cotton of Boston. With this excellent lady he was united more than fifty years, and became the father of ten children; three sons, and seven daughters.

The eldest of these sons, Cotton Mather, was for many years his father's colleague in the ministry, and was, indisputably the most learned man in New England. He was the author of almost four hundred distinct publications, many of them considerable volumes.

Nathaniel Mather, the second son of Increase, died young. He is represented as a very remarkable youth, in respect both to learning and piety. A memoir of him was published by Cotton Mather, which went through several editions, on both sides of the water. A considerable part of the first edition was purchased by good old Philip Henry, for charitable distribution. To the fourth edition, a highly characteristic preface was prefixed by Matthew Mead, author of the "Almost Christian." "I could not read the book," says Mr. Mead, "without great reflection and shame. For, thought I, God will not gather his fruit, till it is ripe; therefore, I live so long. Nor will he let it hang till it is rotten; therefore, Nathaniel Mather died so soon. We are not sent into the world, merely to fill up a *number of years*, but to fill up our *measure of grace*; and whenever that is done, our time is done; we have lived to maturity. And so did this dear youth. Though he died at nineteen, he came to his grave in full age, and fell like a shock of corn in his season."

Samuel Mather, the third and youngest son of Increase, went to England with his father, when he was a child, and seems never to have returned. He became "a faithful and useful minister of the gospel, at Wilney, in Oxfordshire." He was the author of several valuable treatises; among which his "Vindication of the Doctrine of the Trinity," his "Vindication of the Deity of the Holy Spirit," and his "Vindication of the Sacred Scriptures," were the most considerable.

The seven daughters of Increase Mather, (with the exception of one who died in infancy,) all lived to be settled in the world, to have families, and to give decisive evidence of true piety. The whole family were united in the service of Christ in this world, and have long since gone to be forever united around his throne in heaven.

With this brief account, (by way of anticipation) of the family of Increase Mather, we now return to his personal history. He was not inclined, at the first, to be settled over the new church in Boston, nor could his aversion be soon or easily overcome. After an invitation had been extended to him, the people were kept in suspense for more than two years. At length, the brethren of the church carried the matter more publicly and formally to God. They kept a day of fasting and supplication to Him who has all hearts in his hand, imploring that he would turn the heart of the youthful pastor elect, and incline him to accept their invitation. This measure was altogether in accordance with the feelings of Mr. Mather, and an encouragement to him to comply with the people's wishes. He shortly after signified his consent to their proposals, and in May, 1664, was ordained their pastor. And in this situation he continued, serving the Lord "with many tears and temptations, and keeping back nothing that was profitable unto them," for more than sixty years.

In the very commencement of our Saviour's public ministry, he was "led of the Spirit into the wilderness, to be tempted of the devil." And not a few of his faithful disciples have had a similar experience. In the beginning of their ministry, they have suffered bitter temptations from the great adversary. So it was with John Bunyan. "Whole floods of blasphemies," says he, "against God, and Christ, and the holy Scriptures, were poured upon my spirit, to my great confusion and astonishment. These blasphemous thoughts were such as stirred up questions in me against the very being of God, and of his beloved Son; as whether there were, in truth, a God, or Christ, and whether the holy Scriptures were anything more than a cunning story, a fable." *

Those who are familiar with the memoirs of the excellent Dr. Payson, will remember that he

* Ivimey's Life of Bunyan, p. 64.

was sometimes afflicted in a similar way. "O the temptations that have harrassed me for the last three months! I have met with nothing like them in books. I dare not mention them to any mortal, lest they should trouble him, as they have troubled me. But if I should become an apostate, and write against religion, it seems to me that I could bring forward objections which would shake the faith of all the Christians in the world. What I marvel at is, that the arch-deceiver has never been permitted to suggest them to some of his own scribes, and have them published. They would, if I mistake not, make fearful work with Christians for a time, though God would, doubtless, enable them to overcome in the end." *

It is recorded of Richard Baxter, that he was afflicted with the like temptations. And not to multiply instances, the same was true, for a time, of Increase Mather. "The first years of his ministry," says his son, "were embittered with such furious and boisterous temptations unto atheism, as were intolerable to him, and made him cry out, like Peter in the tempest. Vile suggestions, and injections, tending to question the being of that God whom he feared

* Works, vol. I, p. 379.

and loved, and to whom he continually prayed, were shot at him, as fiery darts from the wicked one, and caused him to go mourning because of the oppression of the enemy. His holy soul suffered an intolerable anguish from these blasts of the terrible ones."

The proper inference to be drawn from such cases of temptation is *not* that there is any real *force* or *plausibility* in the objections and arguments of atheists and infidels. The individuals tempted would not so decide, so soon as the delusion had passed away. But the inference rather is, (so the tempted ones understand it, and so the Scriptures represent it,) that there is a mighty malignant spirit, or more properly legions of them, who "go about as roaring lions, seeking whom they may devour." For the *trial* of God's people, they are permitted to have access to their minds, and to worry them, for a time, with their bitter suggestions and their fiery darts. How else, I ask, are such suggestions to be accounted for,—so opposed to the most cherished and established principles of the children of God, so abhorrent to their feelings, so contrary to all their mental associations and habits,—darted too, as they commonly are, into their minds, at seasons and under circumstances when they might least have been expected, and when they are most painful and vexatious? I know not how to account for *facts* of this description,—facts of not unfrequent occurrence, but upon the Scriptural representation as to the existence and agency of evil spirits. And if the suggestions in question proceed from such a source, it certainly is no *recommendation* of them, whether in respect to their reasonableness or their truth.

Mr. Mather's method of repelling atheistical suggestions was not so much in a way of reasoning, as of direct resistance. "It puts too much respect upon the devil," he said, "to argue and parley with him, and that, too, on a point which he himself believes, and for which he trembles. It is too much of a compliment to atheism, to pour in elaborate confutations of it. When we prove anything, we prove what is less known by that which is more known. But is there anything more known, than the existence of a *first cause*, which, in forming the spirit of man, has left on that spirit the impress of itself?"

Instead of trying to reason down atheistical suggestions, Mr. Mather *rejected* them with all possible detestation, as infinitely unworthy to be listened to, and cherished such thoughts only as carried in them the devoutest acknowledgments of a God, and the most fervant supplications to him. In this way, he seems to have tired out the adversary. Being thus resisted, the devil at length fled from him.

These trials, through which Mr. Mather was called to pass in the early part of his ministry, were doubtless necessary for him. They were as necessary as the thorn in the flesh of Paul. As he was a highly popular preacher, whom multitudes flocked together to hear, there was danger of his becoming unduly elated, and thus falling into a worse snare of the devil than that which was laid for him. The temptations to which I have referred, were an effectual means of keeping him humble. He could not but wonder that the people of God should have any esteem for one who was the subject of such abhorred and detestable thoughts, as were sometimes thrust upon himself.

Mr. Mather had trials of another sort in the early part of his ministry, more nearly resembling those of some ministers at the present day. They arose from the inadequacy of his support. After he had been settled a few years, his people, or a *portion* of them, grew slack in the fulfillment of their engagements to him ; in consequence of which he was under the necessity of contracting debts, and involving himself in other embarrassments. The following extracts from his diary in relation to this matter, may fall under the eyes of some who are suffering in the same way. As going to develope his religious character, they will be read with interest by all.

"Extremely grieved and distracted in my studies with the thoughts of my debts, and the consideration that my people, (or some of them,) do not care for my deep sorrows in this respect. Methinks I could be content to be poor, I care not how poor, so as I may be in a capacity to serve God without distraction. But to be in debt, to the dishonor of the gospel, is a wounding, killing thought to me; so grievous, that if it be not remedied in a little time, it will bring me with sorrow to my grave."

Again he writes thus: "Spent this day with prayer and fasting in my study. I closed all with this resolution: 'Lord, if thou wilt provide for me, and answer my prayers, I will love thee, and thank thee, and serve thee. And if thou wilt *not* provide for me, I will yet love thee, and bless thee, and serve thee. If thou wilt cast me off, I will not cast thee off. I deserve that thou shouldest cast me off, but thou, Lord, never deservest ill at my hands.'"

On another day, he writes as follows: "Miserably perplexed with the sad thoughts of my debts, and the unworthy spirit which is in some of my people, who have no heart to relieve me in these my sorrows, and think every thing too much for me; so that I lose (which most of all distresses me,) much precious time, and am exceedingly hindered in the work of the Lord. The Scriptures direct ministers to show themselves fathers of *patience* and *long-suffering*. Conscience of this has made me bear this long; but now I can endure no longer, my grief is so extreme. O that the Lord Jesus, who hears the complaints of his people before him, would condescend to do one of the following things: Either give a heart to my people to look after my comfortable subsistence among them; or remove me to some other people who will take care of me, that so I may be in a capacity to attend to his work, and glorify his name in my generation; or give me a sufficiency of grace, that these sinking discouragements may not overwhelm me; or take me speedily to himself, where no temptation shall keep me from serving him with freedom of spirit. For thy name's sake, Lord Jesus, pity, hear and help."

One part of this prayer seems to have been very soon answered; for in the next published extract from his diary, he writes as follows: "I am now content to be poor, and in debt, and to be laid aside as a broken, useless vessel, if the Lord will have it so. Yea, I am content to be anything that Christ will have me to be. Now I am satisfied; the will of the Lord be done."

And now—the trial having fully answered its purpose in the hand of the great Head of the Church, though without any thanks to those through whose meanness and ingratitude it was inflicted—the time of his deliverance came. The Lord so ordered it that several gentlemen of good estate, and of better spirit, became connected with his church, who "were moved with a just and generous concern, when they learned how their worthy pastor had been treated, and who took effectual care that it should be so no more."

The case of Mr. Mather, as here presented, is an instructive one to us at the present day. Churches and congregations may learn a lesson from it. Little do they think, often, of the sufferings which they inflict upon faithful ministers, by their unkindness and neglect. And as little do they think of the injury which indirectly comes upon themselves. Their ministers cannot serve them, as they otherwise would. They have not the time, the heart, or the capacity to do it. And then the judgments of God often follow in the track of a stinted, cheated, neglected ministry. People "sow much, and bring in little. They eat, but they have not enough. They drink, but they are not satisfied. They clothe themselves, but they are not warm. They earn wages, and put them in a bag, but it is a bag with holes." Hag. 1 : 6.

Ministers also may learn something from the example of Mr. Mather. He was not angry with his people for their neglect of him, but rather pitied them, and prayed for them. "This day, pouring out my complaints into the bosom of the Lord Jesus, I begged of him that he would not punish any of my poor people because of their neglects of me, but pardon them, and bless them."

Again, Mr. Mather was not in haste to break away from his people, and seek another field of labor. "He had offers of a settlement, where he might have mended his condition in the world; but he generously refused it, from a fear lest the way of truth should be evil spoken of." He apprehended, at times, that the day might come when a removal would be necessary, but he would himself do nothing to hasten that day, preferring rather to wait upon the Lord.

The issue of the trial, as before hinted, is

also instructive. So soon as it had answered its appointed purpose, in humbling and silencing the sufferer, and leading him to say with Paul, "I have learned, in whatever state I am, therewith to *be content*," it was kindly and graciously removed, and the day of enlargement and blessing came.

Something has been said already of Mr. Mather's diary. This was less full and copious than that of some Christians of his age; and less so in the latter part of his life than in the earlier. Still, he kept a diary, in which he noted important occurrences, and recorded something of his religious experience. I shall have occasion to speak of the diary again, in a subsequent chapter. At present, I only give some brief extracts from it, illustrative of his religious character.

Mr. Mather usually kept a day of private fasting, once a month, in preparation for the monthly celebration of the Lord's supper. At the close of one of these days, he writes: "My heart was moved to believe that God would accept and answer my prayers, and that for the following reasons: 1. I drew *nigh* to him, and therefore his blessings will draw nigh to me. 2. The things which I asked, and the ends why I asked them, were for the glory of God, and for the honor of his Son Jesus Christ. Not for my own sake, but for the Lord's sake. 3. Nothing but my sins can hinder the answer of my prayers. But these cannot hinder, because they are done away in the blood of Christ, who hath loved me, and given himself for me. Of this I am *sure;* for I feel that my heart loveth him. 4. Never was there any creature who did humbly seek unto the Lord for such blessings as I have this day prayed for, who was denied; and surely I shall not be *the first* to be denied. Forever blessed be my reconciled Father in Christ Jesus, who heareth prayer."

On another of these occasions, he writes: "I put the answer of my prayers upon the sincerity of my soul before God, saying, 'O my God, if I do not sincerely desire to glorify thy name, then deny my requests, and let me have no answer. But if I do in sincerity desire to serve and glorify thee, then have compassion on me, and deny me not. Upon these terms, let me go, either with an answer, or with a denial.' O my soul, wait thou on the Lord."

May 8th, 1672, was set apart by Mr. Mather, as a day of special communion with God, on account of the death of his eldest brother, Samuel, the news of which had just reached him. "In the beginning of the day," he writes, "the

Lord melted my heart. While I was entreating that the Lord would remember the prayers which my precious brother had put up for me, when he was living in the world, and that he would impart much of that spirit to me, which he had caused so eminently to rest on my now blessed, glorified brother;—while I was thus praying, my heart was exceedingly melted, and I had such an inexpressible view of the Divine glory, that I was afraid I should have fainted in my study."

The *public* prayers of Mr. Mather were remarkable for their originality and pertinency, as well as fervor. Extracts from some of them are recorded in his diary,—more especially from those which were offered up at the Lord's table. "I was this day much affected in administering the supper of the Lord, particularly in the last prayer. I said: 'Now, dearest Lord, if ever there were poor creatures in the world who had cause to love and bless the Lord, we are they. We have done thee infinite wrongs; but thou hast forgiven us all these wrongs, and dealest with us as with friends. How can we but mourn for the wrongs that we have done thee? If we had wronged an enemy, and that in a small matter, we should be grieved for it; but we have wronged the Son of God! Have wronged, yea crucified, the Saviour! It was our sins which pierced him on the cross; and the blood which flowed from his wounded body has procured our pardon. O our Father, we have sinned against thee; but we are sorry for it, and would do iniquity no more. Father, forgive us, thou knowest our hearts. Thou knowest that we could rejoice, if we might never have so much as one more sinful thought in our hearts, nor speak so much as one unprofitable word more, whilst we live. Yea, this is the thing that we would most earnestly beg of thee. Deny us not, Lord, this most important request. Let thy Spirit dwell in us, and sanctify us wholly for thyself.'"

We give but another example of these sacramental prayers. "I had some quickenings at the table of the Lord, especially in the last prayer, saying: 'Our heavenly Father, we have avouched thee to be our God, and we believe that thou hast avouched us to be thy people; for thou hast given us thy Son, and thou wilt with him give us all things. Our Father, we do humbly crave of thee, that, according to thy covenant of grace, thou wilt forgive us all our iniquities. Thou wilt not impute our iniquities to us, if they be our burthen; and thou knowest that they are so. We put the answer of our prayers upon this, and are willing to be denied, if it be not so. But thou, who hast searched all our hearts, knowest that thou hast created such a spirit within us. We desire to be delivered from all sin, and to yield a holy obedience to all thy commands ; though how to perform, we find not. Father, deal with us as with thy children.' "

The passages here extracted I am sure will not be unacceptable to the pious reader. They indicate a sweetness and brokenness of spirit, a freedom and intimacy of holy, spiritual communion, which has rarely been equalled, in this world of sin.

It is interesting to know how such a man as Increase Mather ordinarily spent his time. The following method of employing it was adopted in early life, and, with occasional modifications, was continued to the last:

"Lord's day. Besides my public labors, attend to the catechising and personal instruction of my family.

"Monday. Forenoon, read comments ; study sermon. Afternoon, read authors ; study sermon.

"Tuesday. Forenoon, read comments; study sermon. Afternoon, endeavor to instruct *personally* more or less ; read authors.

"Wednesday. Forenoon, read comments; study sermon. Afternoon, read authors; pursue the sermon.

"Thursday. Forenoon, read comments; study sermon. After lecture,* endeavor to promote among the ministers what shall be of public advantage.

"Friday. Forenoon, read comments; study sermon. Afternoon, read authors; finish sermons.

"Saturday. Read comments. Prepare for the Sabbath, by committing my sermons to memory, &c.

"I am not willing to allow myself more than seven hours in twenty-four for sleep, and would spend the rest of my time in attending to the duties of my personal and general calling."

If the above may be regarded as a fair specimen of the manner in which our fathers in the ministry spent their time, then several important facts may be easily accounted for. It is no wonder that they were *mighty in the Scriptures.* Here is Increase Mather studying the Scriptures *six days in the week*, from Monday to Saturday. A part of every forenoon is employed in *reading comments.* These comments were

* Referring to the stated Thursday Lecture.

in different languages, and embraced a vast range of biblical illustration and remark. By this course of study, continued through more than half a century, the language of Scripture became to him as household words, and the interpretation of difficult passages was familiar and easy.

Again; it is not to be wondered at, that the *reading* of our fathers was extensive. Increase Mather literally fulfilled the apostolic injunction, "Give thyself to *reading*." A part of four afternoons in every week, he *read authors*. It is incalculable how many good authors may have been read in this way; and how much the mind may have been enriched; and how well prepared to pour forth its treasures in the stated ministrations of the pulpit.

But especially is it not to be wondered at, that the *sermons* of our fathers were so thoroughly elaborated, and so rich in scriptural, evangelical instruction. Here was Increase Mather *studying his sermons* every day of the week except the Sabbath, and for three days in the week, forenoon and afternoon. He knew what it was to bring *beaten oil* into the sanctuary; nor did he feel at liberty to serve the Lord, or his people with that which cost him little or nothing.

In one respect, Mr. Mather was decidedly in

advance of the ministers of his own age, and perhaps of any other age in New England. I refer to his *manner of delivery*. He was not only a sound and learned divine, but a *graceful and powerful speaker*. He made it an object and labor through life to be so, and he *was* so. He could not consent to be fettered by notes, or to pour forth in the Lord's name, mere extemporary effusions; and so he incurred the labor, habitually, of committing his sermons to memory. Whether or not he was wise in this, I will not now undertake to say; but this I do say, that he was wise in thinking of the *manner* of his sermons, as well as the matter of them, and in studying to make himself an *acceptable and accomplished* preacher, as well as an instructive one. And well had it been for the succeeding ministry of New England, if in this respect he had been more closely imitated.

CHAPTER IV.

Course of Mr. Mather in the controversy respecting infant baptism. His views of religious liberty. His opinions respecting the personal reign of Christ. Death of his father and brother. Severe sickness and recovery.

WHEN Mr. Mather returned from Europe, in 1661, he found the churches and ministers of New England deeply agitated with a controversy respecting the church state of their posterity, and the right of those who were not members in full communion to bring their children to baptism. The older churches had now been established from twenty to thirty years, in which time a generation had risen up, many of whom did not regard themselves as regenerated persons. They were, in general, of sober life, but not having experienced the grace of God in their hearts, they could not in conscience apply for admission to the churches, nor if they had applied, could they have been admitted. The consequence was, that *their* children were not baptized, and were likely to grow up without so much as a nominal connection with the church of Christ. This was a trying emergency to our fathers,—one which they had hardly anticipated; and they were led to look about them and inquire, "*What shall be done?* Will it be safe to innovate on the established order of the churches, and admit persons to communion, without a credible profession of piety? Or will it be safe to shut our posterity out of the church, deprive them of the privilege of Christian ordinances, and in this way expose the cherished vine, which, with so many prayers and tears, we have planted in the wilderness, to an early decay and an ultimate desolation?" These trying questions were first started in Connecticut; and we cannot well conceive of the feeling and interest with which they soon forced themselves upon the attention of the colonies. They were discussed and decided at a meeting of ministers in Boston, in 1657. They were also decided in a general synod, in 1662. In these decisions, which were substantially the same, the difficulty was rather evaded than removed. It was not determined that persons of sober life who gave no evidence of piety, should be admitted to the church; nor was it determined that they could hold *no sort* of connection with the church, and that their children must remain unbaptized. A middle course was suggested and adopted ; viz : " that it is the duty of those who have been baptized in infancy, when grown to years of discretion, though not yet fit for the Lord's supper, to *own the covenant* made on their behalf by their parents, by entering into it in their own persons ; and it is the duty of the church to *call* upon them for the performance thereof. And if, being called upon, they shall refuse to perform this duty, or otherwise continue scandalous, they are liable to be censured for the same by the church. But if they understand the grounds of religion, and are not scandalous, and solemnly own the covenant in their own persons, wherein they give up both themselves and their children unto the Lord, and desire baptism for them, we see no reason why such children are not to be baptized."

Such was the origin of infant baptism, on the ground of what has been denominated "the *half-way covenant*." It was an innovation on the original platform of the New England churches, which, though sanctioned by a synod, and recommended by the general court, was not adopted without long controversy. Mr. Mather was at this time a young man; but he united his efforts with those of President Chauncy and the venerable John Davenport, in opposition to the measure; though, through the influence of his father, and of his particular friend, Mr. Mitchell of Cambridge, he was afterwards led to adopt it.

The result of the expedient, however, was disastrous. Its tendency was to enfeeble and secularize the church, while it quieted the consciences of many who were living in acknowledged impenitence, without hope and without God in the world. Most persons of sober life, when they came to have families, "owned the covenant," and presented their children for baptism; but the number of church members in *full communion*, was diminishing. Baptism was administered to great multitudes, but the Lord's Supper, the other special ordinance of the gospel, was falling rather into neglect.

If on this question of infant baptism Mr. Mather changed his opinions for the worse, I may notice another instance in which he changed them for the better; and in which he seems to have led the way to a more liberal and scriptural mode of thinking than had before prevailed in New England. As our fathers came to this land almost entirely from religious considerations,—that they might establish churches after what they conceived to be the Divine pattern, and maintain the faith and order of the gospel, so they were very unwilling, more especially in the earlier part of the settlement, to be disturbed. If those who essentially differed from them sought here an asylum for their peculiarities, "the world," they said, "is wide. You are at liberty to turn to the right hand, or the left; but you must not intrude here, to disturb us. If you cannot think and walk with us, we prefer you should walk to some other section of the country." It is perfectly natural, that a feeling such as this should have prevailed among the early settlers of New England. Their peculiar circumstances furnished an excuse for it, if they did not create a necessity. The feeling did not prevail to the extent that many have pretended; still, there was something of it here. "Hence," says Cotton Mather, "toleration was decried, as a Trojan horse, profanely and perilously brought into the city of God. Plausible outcries were made about Anti-Christ's coming in at the back door of toleration. It was also a maxim often cited, that *to tolerate all things, and tolerate nothing, are both alike intolerable.*"

It was natural that Mr. Mather, in the first part of his ministry, should fall in with these current and established opinions. It is even said that he wrote a book, which was never published, on the power of the magistrate to restrain and subdue heretical doctrines. But as he advanced in years, his views on this subject underwent a material change. He became entirely tolerant in his principles, and advocated religious freedom, much as it is understood at the present day. He insisted "that the man who is a good neighbor, and a good subject, has a right to his life and the comforts of it; and that it is not his being of this or that opinion in religion, but *his doing of something which directly tends to the hurt of human society*, by which this right can be forfeited. He saw that a good neighbor and a good subject has a claim to all his temporal enjoyments *before* he is a Christian; and he thought it very odd that a man should lose this claim from his embracing Christianity, just because he does not happen to be a Christian of the uppermost party among the subdivisions. He saw, in short, that until persecutions be utterly banished out of the world, and Cain's club be taken out of Abel's hand, as well as out of Cain's, it is impossible to rescue the world from endless confusions."

It is sometimes thought that the principles of Christian liberty are of recent discovery. But where shall we look for a more explicit statement and striking illustration of them, than in the foregoing passages? And yet these were the settled and recorded principles of Increase

Mather, almost two hundred years ago;—principles on which he uniformly and consistently acted. At an early period, he assisted in ordaining the pastor of a Baptist church in his immediate neighborhood; and Cotton Mather, speaking of the state of things in New England at a later period, says: "Calvinists with Lutherans, Presbyterians with Episcopalians, Pedobaptists with Anabaptists, beholding one another *to fear God and work righteousness*, do with delight sit down together at the same table of the Lord; nor do they hurt one another in the holy mountain."

As we are now upon the opinions of Increase Mather, it may be proper to notice a point in which he agreed, substantially, with his cotemporaries, but differed from the generality of Christians at the present day. The opinions now prevailing in this country in respect to the Millennium, date not much further back than the time of President Edwards. It was his discussions of the subject, together with those of Doctors Hopkins and Bellamy, which changed the previously received notions of the Millennium, for those which now so generally prevail. The first ministers of New England, like many of the primitive Christians, and of the Protestant reformers, lived in habitual expectation of the second coming of Christ. Some thought, with Wickliffe, that the Millennium was past, and that they were living in the very last days of the world. Others held that the Millennium was about to be ushered in by the second coming of Christ, to reign personally and gloriously on the earth, during the whole of that period. In proof that such opinions very generally prevailed, I might adduce many facts. Thus, at the time of the great earthquake in New England, in the year 1727, multitudes mistook the roar of it for the sounding of the last trump, supposing that Christ had already come. It was followed by a great awaking in Boston, though not, as we are informed, by many conversions. Also, during certain vivid and terrific corruscations of the Aurora Borealis, which occurred more than a hundred years ago, many excellent people walked the streets the whole night, expecting the instant appearance of the Son of Man.

As might be expected, Mr. Mather adopted and advocated the current opinions respecting the speedy coming of Christ, and was, without doubt, a means of extending and establishing them. About the year 1668, he wrote a book, in Latin, which was afterwards published in Holland, entitled "A Diatribe concerning the Sign of the Son of Man, and the Second Coming of the Messiah;" in which he insists that this great event "will be at *the beginning* of that happy state which is to be expected for the church on earth, in the latter days."

In the spring of 1669, Mr. Mather was called to bury his father, and scarcely had this sad office of affection and piety been performed, when tidings reached him of the sudden death of his beloved brother Eleazer. This made it necessary for him to take a journey to Northampton, that he might assist and comfort the desolate widow and the afflicted people. While here, he was himself attacked with a violent fever, which continued many days. During this period, he was the subject of incessant prayer, and a physician was sent all the way from Boston to his relief. He recovered slowly, and was but just able to return to his family and people before the setting in of winter. He was kept from his pulpit by continued weakness and indisposition, till the next spring. During his sickness, he wrote as follows:

"God was wonderfully gracious to me. He did not leave me to doubts and fears, but caused his face to shine upon me. I found myself very willing to die. When I thought of my wife and children, my heart gave them up to God, firmly believing that he would take care of them.

I had as much quiet in my mind, as though I had neither wife nor child to care for. When I thought of that blessedness which is to be enjoyed in another world, I longed to be there. O the presence of God! The presence of God! It is sweeter than life itself. My soul knoweth it."

In the spring of the year 1670, we find Mr. Mather again in the pulpit. His first sermon was from these words: "Blessed is the man whom thou chastenest, O Lord, and teachest out of thy law." Still, however, he was feeble in body, and in a somewhat melancholy and hypochondriac state of mind. On one occasion, he records his feelings to this effect: "I was in much distress and anguish of spirit, lest all my faith should prove but phantasy and delusion. In this trouble, I betook myself to Christ, and wept before him, saying, 'Lord Jesus, let me be destroyed, if thou canst find it in thy heart to destroy a poor creature, who desires, above all things, to glorify thy name. Here I am before thee. Do *to* me and *with* me, as thou wilt. If thou wilt glorify thyself in my confusion, thy will be done. I have deserved that it should be so. But O that thou wouldest hear me, and pity me!' After I had thus fled and cried unto the Rock of my Salvation, I was revived."

As soon as Mr. Mather was able to engage in such a labor, we find him preparing and publishing a Memoir of his father. He also prepared for the press and published a volume of his brother Eleazer's sermons. They were intended especially for the rising generation, and had a wide circulation among the youth of New England.

CHAPTER V.

Philip's war. Great fire in Boston. Small Pox. The reforming Synod. Mr. Mather's agency in it. Severe fits of sickness. Ordination of his Son. Is appointed President of Harvard College.

For the next four or five years after Mr. Mather's recovery from sickness, he seems to have devoted himself, with more quiet and constancy than usual, to the concerns of his flock. The year 1675 was one of great terror and distress in New England. Instigated by Philip, a chief of the Narragansetts, most of the Indians in the country (with the exception of those who had been converted to Christianity,) entered into a conspiracy to cut off the white inhabitants, or drive them from the land. To effect this object, Philip is said to have had in the field, at one time, an army of three thousand warriors. And when it is considered that these savages were athletic, cunning, treacherous, cruel, perfectly acquainted with localities, expert in the use of firearms with which they were now well supplied, and capable of enduring hunger and hardship to any requisite amount, it will be seen, at once, that three thousand of them, under charge of such a leader as Philip, must have been a most terrible body to the New England settlers. As this was the last *general* war with the Indians, so it was the most bloody and desolating of them all. It continued nearly two years, in which time many flourishing towns were reduced to ashes, and not less than six hundred of the English settlers, constituting the flower and strength of several of the districts, either fell in battle, or were massacred in their dwellings, or expired under the tortures and hardships of an Indian captivity.

Mr. Mather warned his people, and the country, of the approaching day of trouble, before it came; and when it did come, he made the best use of it, by bearing solemn testimony against those prevailing iniquities which had provoked the judgments of heaven, and in calling his suffering fellow citizens to repentance. As the people were unable, during these years of terror, to cultivate their fields with safety and success, the country was threatened with the horrors of famine, as well as those of war. In this extremity, Mr. Mather, "by his letters, procured a whole ship's load of provisions from the charity of his friends in Dublin, and a considerable sum of money and much clothing, from friends in

London, to be distributed among the needy and distressed." Our country is at *this time* paying a debt of gratitude, so long ago contracted, by sending back *ship-loads* of provisions to the starving and perishing in Ireland and England.

In the year 1676, (the second year of Philip's war,) Boston was visited with a distressing fire. In some unaccountable way, Mr. Mather had a presentiment of the approach of this calamity, and warned his people of it, two Sabbaths in succession. The very night of the second Sabbath, the fire broke out in his immediate neighborhood, his meeting-house and dwelling-house were both consumed, and whole streets were laid in ashes. His library, which was in part consumed, was soon made up to him by the generosity of friends; and in less than two years he was put in possession of a better house than that he had lost. His flock was scattered for a time, till a place of worship could be provided; but "God made it an opportunity for him to preach every Lord's day in the other churches, and thus to benefit the whole city with his enlightening and awakening ministry."

Only two years after, New England was visited with another distressing calamity—*the small pox.* As neither vaccination nor inoculation was then practiced, we can hardly conceive of the terror and distress which such a visitation must have inflicted on the suffering inhabitants. It was like the plague or the cholera of our own times ; and even *more* distressing, as the disease was more fearfully contagious. Never before had Boston seen so dreadful a mortality. "The cry of the city went up to heaven."

These repeated and sore corrections led our fathers to look around them, and to search their own hearts and characters, for the cause. They remembered that long promulged maxim of the Divine government: "If his children forsake my law, and walk not in my judgments; if they break my statutes, and keep not my commandments, then will I visit their transgressions with a rod, and their iniquity with stripes ;" and they were led very carefully to inquire wherein they had forsaken the law and the judgments of God, broken his statutes and commandments, and thereby exposed themselves to such awful visitations.

"New England," says Cotton Mather, "was not become, at this time, so degenerate a country but that there was yet preserved in it far more of serious religion, as well as of blameless morality, than was proportionably to be seen in any country upon the face of the earth. Nevertheless, the spirit of the world had begun so far to operate, that there was a visible decay of real and vital piety, and the power of godliness had sensibly suffered some abatements. Watchful, fruitful, prayerful Christians, and humble walkers with God, were not so many as they had been, among a people greatly multiplying, and the holy God might also say, "There are wicked men among my people."

Wherefore, upon the suggestion of Mr. Mather and others, the general court convoked a synod, (commonly called the reforming synod,) to consist of pastors and delegates from the several churches of the colony, whose duty it should be to consider and report upon the following questions:

1. What are the evils that have provoked the Lord to bring his judgments upon New England?

2. What is to be done, that so these evils may be reformed?

The churches having first kept a general fast, that the blessing of God might rest upon the proposed undertaking, the synod met at Boston, September 10, 1679. The first day of the session was spent in prayer and fasting, in the course of which Mr. Mather and old Mr. Cobbett of Ipswich preached. Several days were then occupied in a free discussion of the questions proposed; after which a result, drawn up by Mr. Mather, was unanimously adopted. On the day when this result was presented to the general court, Mr. Mather preached again, on "the Danger of not being Reformed by these Things." The result was cordially accepted by the court, and commended to "the serious consideration of all the churches and people in the jurisdiction."

Among the *evils* enumerated by the synod as having provoked the judgments of God, were the following: 1. A great and visible decay of the power of godliness among professors of religion. 2. Abounding pride. 3. Profaneness. 4. Sabbath-breaking. 5. Neglecting family government. 6. The indulgence of inordinate passions. 7. Intemperance. 8. Violations of honesty and truth. 9. An inordinate love of the world. 10. A want of public spirit. 11. Sins more directly against the gospel. 12. A manifest unwillingness to be reformed.

In answer to the second question, viz: What things are to be done, that so these evils may be removed; the synod recommend, 1. That the work of reformation commence with magistrates, and all those who are in authority. "Moses, being to reform others, began with what concerned himself and his. People are apt to follow the example of those that are above them.'

2. The synod recommend a public declaration of adherence to the Cambridge Platform of church order and discipline. This recommendation was carried into effect in the synod itself; every member lifting his hand in favor of the Platform, and not one appearing against it. 3. The synod enjoin greater strictness and faithfulness in the admission of members to the churches; also in maintaining church discipline. 4. The synod further recommend the most earnest endeavors for supplying the churches with faithful pastors, and for their encouragement and support in fulfilling the duties of their office. 5. A reformation may be much promoted by due care and faithfulness in the establishment and execution of wholesome laws. 6. Solemn and explicit renewal of covenant is a scriptural expedient for reformation. 7. Effectual care must be taken to establish and encourage schools of learning. Finally, "it becometh us to cry mightily unto God, both in an ordinary and extraordinary manner, that he would be pleased to rain down righteousness upon us."

I have presented this abstract of the doings of the famous reforming synod, as illustrating not only the spirit of the times, but the personal character and history of Mr. Mather. As he originated the project of a synod, so he was the prime mover and counselor in all its deliberations. The result which, as before stated, was drawn up by his hand, gives evidence of his diligence in searching out existing evils, and of his unsparing fidelity in directing to the most appropriate remedies.

The synod itself, if it did not accomplish all that was expected, was of essential service to the cause of piety. Encouraged and strengthened by it, ministers were more searching and faithful in their discourses, and their labors were followed with a proportionally increased success. The best effects were also realized from that *renewal of covenant* which the synod so earnestly recommended. The churches first came together, with their pastors, to consider what God expected of them, and to prepare their minds for the solemn service in which they were about to engage. Then, on a day set apart for the service, and after appropriate sermons and prayers, the proposed covenant was read to them, and all united in receiving and adopting it. And as there was usually a multitude of people present on these occasions, so there were thousands who felt and testified that they never saw more convincing evidence of the special presence of God, than was witnessed in these awful solemnities.

The synod of which we have spoken had a

8*

second session in the spring of the following year, at which time Mr. Mather was appointed moderator. It was at this session, that the New England Confession of Faith was adopted. This is the same as the Savoy Confession; and substantially the same, as to the doctrinal parts of it, with the more celebrated Westminster Confession. The reason why our fathers preferred to *adopt* a confession already in existence, rather than prepare one for themselves, was, as they inform us, that by agreeing to the very "words of their brethren in England, they might, with one *mouth* as well as heart, glorify God and our Lord Jesus Christ."

At a general court held in Boston, May 19, 1680, the result of the second session of synod, then just closed, was presented for acceptance, whereupon the following order was passed: "This court, having taken into consideration the request that hath been presented by several of the reverend elders, in the name of the late synod, do approve thereof; and accordingly order, that the Confession of faith agreed upon, together with the Platform of discipline consented unto by the synod at Cambridge in 1648, be printed, for the benefit of the churches in present and after times."

Mr. Mather was ill when the second session

of the synod commenced, of which he was appointed moderator; but so intent was he on the business to be done, that for the time he forgot his sickness; and so closely did he keep his brethren to their work, that in two days they despatched it, and were ready to return to their homes.

On this, Mr. Mather immediately took his bed, under a dangerous fever, which left him with a cough, and with symptoms of consumption. He was sick a long time, was brought very low, and his life at times despaired of. When inquired of whether he expected soon to die, he answered: "I am not careful about that matter. I have the consciousness that I have *endeavored* to walk before God with a perfect heart, and to do that which is well pleasing in his sight. Nevertheless, I do not think I shall die of this sickness. I have not yet suffered for my Lord Jesus Christ so much as I have desired. Much prayer was offered up by his church and by other Christian friends, on his behalf; and upon his recovery, his people did him the honor to observe a day of public *thanksgiving*, for so great a favor.

In the year 1681, the Rev. Urian Oakes, President of Harvard College, died, and Mr. Mather was appointed his successor. At the commencement following, he took the chair and conferred the degrees; but as his church were unwilling to grant him a dismission, the office was at length declined.

In the year 1684, Mr. Mather had another severe fit of sickness, during which (as before,) much prayer was offered up to God for him, and he was favored with a calm serenity of mind, rejoicing in hope of the glory to be revealed. His first sermon after his recovery was from Is. 38: 18, 19. "The grave cannot praise thee. The living, the living, he shall praise thee, as I do this day." The leading sentiment of the discourse was this: "The servants of God, whilst living in the world, have many opportunities and advantages to glorify him, which the saints in heaven have not." Among other particulars, this was noticed; "they have the opportunity to *suffer* for him."

It was during this year, that Mr. Mather had the satisfaction of receiving his son, Cotton Mather, as his colleague in the work of the ministry. The son was ordained May 13, 1684, when his father preached. Messrs. Allen and Willard, in connection with his father, imposed hands, and the venerable Eliot expressed the fellowship of the churches. The connection thus formed between father and son was continued, with the utmost harmony, (except that the father was occasionally absent,) for almost forty years.

After the death of President Rogers, in 1685, Mr. Mather was again requested "to act as President of the college, until a further settlement be made;" with the understanding that he was to reside and preach in Boston, and spend a portion of his time at Cambridge during the week. In this way, his *official* connection with the college commenced; and it continued without any material alteration (except that he afterwards became, not merely the *acting*, but the *actual* President) for a period of about sixteen years.

Up to this time, the classes at Cambridge had usually consisted of from two, three, or four students up to eight or ten. But during the presidency of Mr. Mather, the number increased, so that the classes often consisted of more than twenty. In the year 1682, a new college edifice was erected, denominated Harvard Hall, which stood till it was destroyed by fire, in 1764. The sixteen years of Mr. Mather's presidency was a deeply interesting period, not only to the college, but also to the colonies, to both of which he sustained the most important relations. A review of it will be undertaken in the following chapters.

CHAPTER VI.

The charter of Massachusetts demanded. Mr. Mather dissuades from surrendering it. Rage of his enemies. The charter taken away. Death of Charles II., and accession of James. Provisional government established. Administration of Sir Edmund Andros. Mr. Mather sent to England on an agency for the colony.

We have heard already of the Reforming Synod of 1679,—of its occasion, and results. It was hoped that a reformation and return to God so general and entire would be effected, that the tokens of his displeasure against the people of New England might be removed. But it was soon manifest that his holy hand was stretched out still, and that trials and perils more formidable than any that our fathers had yet encountered were before them.

From the accession of Charles II. to this time, a period of some ten or twelve years, there had never been a good understanding between him and the New England colonies, more especially that of Massachusetts. From time to time, he had been pressing claims upon the colonists, which they had endeavored to evade, and had been making encroachments upon their chartered liberties, which they were determined to resist. Prejudiced individuals (foremost among whom was the notorious Edward Randolph,) were also filling the royal ears with complaints against the colonies, and increasing the causes of irritation, by every method in their power. At length, in October, 1683, Randolph came over with a message from the king, that unless the people of Massachusetts would make a full submission and entire resignation of their charter to his pleasure, a *Quo Warranto* against it should be prosecuted. The question before the people was, whether they should voluntarily surrender their charter, or have it forcibly taken from them. This question was submitted to Mr. Mather, who in his answer demonstrated that they would act the part, neither of true Englishmen nor of good Christians, if, by any act of theirs, they became accessory to the plot then in progress to produce a general shipwreck of their liberties. This answer was instantly and widely circulated, and with great effect; and in proportion to its effects was the rage of Randolph, and those who acted under his influence. In the fullness of their spite, they customarily spoke of Mr. Mather as the Mahomet of New England. Still, the good man was not to be terrified or deterred from discharging what he believed his duty. Accordingly, when the freemen of Boston came together to give instructions to their deputies to the general court, he was desired to be present, and to favor them with his thoughts on the case of conscience that was to come before them. The speech which he made in the town-house on that occasion is preserved, and is *verbatim* as follows: "Gentlemen, as the question is now stated, whether you will make a full submission and entire resignation of your charter, and the privileges of it, unto his majesty's pleasure, I verily believe we shall sin against the God of heaven, if we vote an affirmative to it. The Scripture teacheth us otherwise. We know what Jephthah said, 'That which the Lord our God has given us, shall we not possess it?' And though Naboth ran a great hazard by the refusal, yet he said, 'God forbid that I should give away the inheritance of my fathers.' Nor would it be *wisdom* for us to comply. We know that David made a wise choice, when he preferred to fall into the hands of God, rather than into the hands of men. If we make a full submission and entire resignation to the king's pleasure, we fall directly into the hands of men. But if we do it not, we still keep ourselves in the hands of God. We trust ourselves with his providence; and who knows what God may do for us? There are also examples before our eyes, the consideration of which should have weight with us. Our brethren hard by us, what have they gained by being so ready to part with their liberties, but an acceleration of their miseries?* And we hear from London, that the loyal citizens would not make a full submission and entire resignation, lest their posterity should curse them for it. And shall *we*, then, do such a thing? I hope there is not a freeman in Boston that can be guilty of it. However, I have discharged my conscience in what I have thus declared to you."

This speech was received with great satisfaction by the freemen of Boston. Many of them were affected to tears, and all came round him with expressions of gratitude. But Randolph and his party were more enraged than ever; and one method which they took to injure Mr. Mather, is too strongly characteristic of them to be wholly passed over. They forged a letter in the name of Mr. Mather, and caused it to be put into the hands of Sir Lionel Jenkins, the king's Secretary of State, containing severe reflections upon the Secretary, and praising certain individuals who were known to be obnoxious to the

* Referring, doubtless, to the Plymouth colony, which was without a charter.

king. The forgery, however, was so palpable, that the secretary treated it with contempt.—When Mr. Mather heard of it, he wrote at once to the secretary, disclaiming all knowledge of the letter, and expressing the opinion that Randolph wrote it. This excited the hatred of Randolph the more, and he brought two successive actions against Mr. Mather for defamation. But from both of them the good man escaped; in the first instance, by being honorably acquitted; and in the second, as we shall see, by being sent out of the country.

But to return to the charter. The people having refused to surrender it, the process of *quo warranto* was urged forward with all the expedition that was compatible with forensic formality. Among other instances of tyrannical contempt of justice, the summons which required the colony to defend itself was transmitted so tardily, that before compliance with it was possible, the space assigned for such compliance had elapsed. In the year 1684, judgment was pronounced against the charter by the English court of King's Bench, and in July of the following year, an official copy of this judgment was received in Boston.

No sooner had judgment been rendered against the charter, than Charles began to make arrangements for the new government of the colony. "And as if he purposed to consummate his tyranny and vengeance by a measure that should surpass the darkest anticipations entertained in New England, he selected as the delegate of his prerogative, a man, than whom it would be difficult, in all the records of human wickedness and oppression to find *one* who has excited to a greater degree the abhorrence and indignation of his fellow creatures. The notorious Col. Kirke, whose ferocious and detestable cruelty has secured him an immortality of infamy in the history of old England, was appointed governor of Massachusetts, New Hampshire, Maine, and New Plymouth; and it was determined that no representative assembly of the colonists, should be permitted to exist, but that all the functions of municipal authority should be vested in the governor, and a council appointed during the royal pleasure."*

In these days of trial and peril to New England, the pious ministers and churches had no resource but in prayer; and here they had a resource and a consolation, of which their enemies were ignorant. The following record is in Mr. Mather's diary of Feb. 6th, 1685. "This

* Grahame's Hist. of U. States, vol. I, p. 255.

day, as I was praying to God for the deliverance of New England, I was very much moved and melted before the Lord, so that for sometime I was not able to speak a word. And then, I could not but say, and repeat, 'God *will* deliver New England! God *will* deliver New England!' So I rose from my knees with much comfort and assurance that God had heard me. Before I prayed, I was very sad, and much dejected in my spirit; but after I had prayed, I was very cheerful and joyful. I will therefore wait for the salvation of God." Thus wrote Mr. Mather on the sixth of February; and in the course of a few weeks it was ascertained, than on that very day king Charles died, and the coming of Kirke on his bloody errand to this country was entirely defeated. This ruthless ruffian was thus retained in England, to contribute by his sanguinary violence there to bring hatred and exile on Charles' successor. *Verily, there is a God that heareth prayer* And the examples illustrative of this, occurring in our own early history, are scarcely exceeded by those recorded in the Scriptures.

Charles II. was succeeded by his brother, James II., from whose stern, inflexible temper and lofty ideas of royal prerogative, the most gloomy presages of tyranny were derived.

With melancholy solemnity he was proclaimed at Boston, in April, 1685.

Soon after his accession, he appointed a *provisional* government for the provinces of Massachusetts, New Hampshire, Maine, and New Plymouth, to be composed of a President and council selected from the inhabitants, whose functions were to continue till the establishment of a fixed and permanent system. At the head of this government was placed Joseph Dudley, a native of Massachusetts, who hitherto had enjoyed the favor of the citizens, but who from this time became, deservedly, an object of suspicion.

It was the misfortune of the provisional government to give satisfaction to neither party. The colonists were indignant, to behold a system which had been erected on the ruin of their liberties administered by one of their own native born citizens; while the king and his party (among whom was Randolph,) thought Dudley not sufficiently careful to carry out their schemes of arbitrary power. This government, therefore, was soon superseded; and a governor and council were appointed by the king, who were to unite in themselves all legislative and executive authority. Kirke had been found too useful, as an instrument of terror in England, to be spared out of it; and so Sir Edmund Andros was appointed governor of the colonies. Dudley, the late President, was one of his council, and the infamous Edward Randolph, was his secretary. The administration of Andros continued a little more than two years; and as he and his council were entrusted with arbitrary powers, so most arbitrarily did they use them. The writers of that day, when speaking of the course pursued, seem to lose all patience, and to labor for words in which to set forth adequately their sense of injury and of reprobation. "It would make a long and black story," says Cotton Mather, "to tell a tenth part of the vile things done by that scandalous crew, who then did what they pleased in the administration of the government. The honest members of the council were overlooked, brow-beaten, and rendered insignificant. Three or four finished villains did what they pleased; there was no controlling of them."

If any are disposed to abate somewhat from this representation, on the ground of excited feeling, we shall find that sober historians of a later day give us substantially the same account. "The weight of taxation," says Mr. Grahame, "was oppressively augmented, and the fees of all public functionaries screwed up to an enormous height. The ceremonial of marriage was altered, and the celebration of that rite confined to ministers of the church of England, of whom there was only one in the whole province of Massachusetts. The fasts and thanksgivings appointed by the churches, were suppressed by the governor, who maintained that the regulation of such matters belonged entirely to the civil power. He took occasion to remark repeatedly, and with the most offensive insolence, in presence of the council, that the colonists would find themselves mistaken, if they supposed that the privileges of Englishmen followed them to the ends of the earth; and that the only difference between their condition and that of slaves was, that they were not bought and sold. It was declared unlawful for the people to assemble in public meetings, or for any one to quit the province without a passport from the governor; and Randolph, now at the summit of his wishes, was not ashamed to boast in his private letters, that he and the governor were '*as arbitrary as the Great Turk.*' While Andros mocked the people with the semblance of trial by jury, he contrived, by intrigue and partiality in the selection of jurymen, to wreak his vengeance on every person who offended him, and to screen the misdeeds of his own dependants from the punishment which they deserved. And, as if to heighten the discontent excited by such tyrannical proceedings, he took occasion to question the validity of the existing land titles, pretending that the rights acquired under the sanction of the old charter, were tainted with its vices and obnoxious to its fate. New grants or patents from the governor, it was announced, were requisite to mend the defective titles to land; and writs of intrusion were issued against all who refused to apply for such patents, and to pay the exhorbitant fees that were charged for them."

It was at this juncture that Sir William Phipps, a native and a devoted friend of New England, undertook to do something for the suffering colonists. Being a personal friend of James II., and now present at his court, he procured for himself the office of high-sheriff of New England; in the hope that, by remedying the abuses that were committed in the empanneling of juries, he might create a barrier against the tyranny of Andros. But the governor and his creatures, incensed at this interference, hired ruffians to attack Sir William Phipps, and soon compelled him to quit the country. In short, our fathers of that day were not only called to give up their estates, but they were led seriously to consider whether their lives would be long secure.

In the midst of all this distress and alarm, the people at length determined to send an agent to England, to lay their case at the feet of their Sovereign, and to implore protection and relief. And in looking round for a suitable person to whom to commit this responsible agency, all eyes seemed to rest on Mr. Mather. When the question of his going was submitted to him, he did as he was wont to do in similar cases: First, he carried the matter to God; and, secondly, to his church. The question was brought before the church in the following terms: "If you say to me, *stay*, I will stay; but if you say, *go*, I will cast myself on the providence of God, and in his name I will go. I know not how to discern the mind of God, but by your inclinations." And to his surprise—such was the distress of the times, and the urgency of the occasion—his people unanimously consented to his departure. The probability is, that they had begun to have fears for his life, if he remained; and they hoped that he might be an instrument of some deliverance to a land, that was in a way to be overthrown and made desolate by strangers.

But how was Mr. Mather to go? The government, with all its facilities and resources, was in the hands of tyrants, who, so far from aiding, would certainly frustrate the proposed agency, if it lay in their power. The government *did* exert itself to the utmost to hinder Mr. Mather from going. It was to stop him, that the second action was brought against him for defaming Randolph in charging upon him the authorship of the forged letter ; but his friends secreted him from his pursuers, and at last sent him out of the country in disguise.

CHAPTER VII.

Mr. Mather arrives at London. Interviews with king James. Revolution in England, and in this country. Interviews with king William, and queen Mary. Despairs of the restoration of the former charter. Obtains a new one. Other services in England. Returns to Boston with Governor Phipps.

Mr. Mather arrived at London, May 25, 1688, in high hope that he should soon be able to effect something for his suffering countrymen. Five days afterwards, he had an interview with king James, and presented the address of his constituents, which was graciously accepted. Mr. Mather had four other meetings with the king, in the course of as many months, in all which, he received an abundance of good words and fair speeches, but nothing more. Indeed, it is highly probable, that while the king was putting off Mr. Mather with delusive promises, saying, "What you desire, sir, is reasonable; *it shall be done*, and *done speedily*;" he was actually plotting, as he admitted in one of his letters to the Pope, "to set up the Roman Catholic religion in the English provinces of North America."

But the intrigues, the deceptions and usurpations of James, were of short continuance. In November of this same year, (1688,) the happy revolution commenced, which exiled the reigning monarch, and placed William and Mary on the throne.

This revolution in the mother country, was immediately followed by the overthrow of Andros' government in Massachusetts. The people rose *en masse;* took possession of an armed frigate, which had been stationed in Boston harbor, with a view to overawe them; seized Andros, Dudley, Randolph, and some fifty of their oppressors, and committed them to prison; established a temporary government, according to the provisions of the old charter, to be continued until advices should be received from England; replaced the venerable Governor Bradstreet, and the other magistrates, in the several offices from which they had been driven; and revived throughout, so far as they were able, the former civil condition of the colony. Never was revolution more complete and satisfactory; and all accomplished without violence—without the shedding of one drop of blood.

In the month following, William and Mary

were joyfully proclaimed in Boston; and shortly after a letter was received from them, expressing the royal sanction of the late proceedings in Massachusetts, and authorizing the present magistrates to retain the administration of the provincial government, until their Majesties, with the assistance of the privy council, should establish it on a more permanent basis. An order was at the same time communicated, to send Andros and the other prisoners to England, that they might answer to the charges preferred against them. Two additional agents, Messrs. Elisha Cook, and Thomas Oakes, were deputed by the colony to join Mr. Mather in England, and endeavor, with him, to promote the interests of the colonies.

Before the arrival of Messrs. Cook and Oakes, Mr. Mather had two interviews with King William, on the subject of a renewal of the vacated charter. To effect this object, he also contrived to get a bill before Parliament, which actually passed the House of Commons. Great interest was made in the upper house, that when the bill should be received, it might be regarded with favor there. But before it could be carried through, Parliament was dissolved, and Mr. Mather had the mortification to find, that all his labor, thus far, had come to nothing.

It was soon evident, from the disposition of the next Parliament, that no favor was to be expected from it for New England. Mr. Mather's next attempt was to bring the matter before the courts, and effect his object through their instrumentality; but here again he was defeated. Despairing now of the restoration of the former charter, the agents of the colony bent all their endeavors to the procuring of a *new one*, which should be acceptable to the people. In this, they were greatly assisted by several of the nobility; such as Archbishop Tillotson, Bishop Burnet, the Earl of Monmouth, and especially the venerable Lord Wharton, the last surviving member of the famous Westminster Assembly. Archbishop Tillotson told the king, that "it would not look well for him to take from the good people of New England any of those privileges which Charles I. had granted them." Lord Wharton said to his majesty; "If I were sure to die tomorrow, I would, as I now do, appear in behalf of New England, and solicit your favor to that religious country. The inhabitants of that country are a godly, conscientious people. There are proportionably more good men there, than in any part of the world. They do not ask your majesty for money, or for soldiers, or for any succors of this sort under their heavy difficulties, but merely for such a charter as shall secure their ancient privileges." During the king's absence in Holland, Mr. Mather had a long and highly satisfactory interview with the queen, who consented herself to write to her husband in behalf of New England.

At length, after immense labor, and frequent disappointments and delays, the promised charter was finished, and put into the hands of the agents of the colony. And now another question arose: Whether the agents should accept the charter, or whether they should signify to the ministers of state, that they rather preferred no charter at all, than such an one as had been given them. This question was the more embarrassing, because the agents were divided in opinion respecting it.

As very much depended on the judgment of Mr. Mather, he was careful to act with deliberation. He took advice of many judicious persons, noblemen, gentlemen, divines, lawyers—men to be depended on as true friends of New England, who all said to him: "Take the proposed charter, and be thankful for it. If it is not every thing you wish, it is the best you can obtain, and altogether safer and better for you than none." Such was the opinion of Sir Henry Ashurst, and Sir William Phipps, who, though not formally connected with the agency, were as deeply interested for New England as those who were. Such was the opinion of Mr. Mather; and such was supposed to be the opinion of a large majority of the people of Massachusetts. They had suffered too much from the mere pleasure of a king, to be willing to trust it any farther, and preferred a *written guaranty* of their rights and privileges, although the instrument might not be in all respects such as they would themselves have dictated. With great deference, therefore, the charter was accepted, though in opposition to the wishes of Messrs. Cook and Oakes; and as the king granted to the agents the privilege of nominating the first governor, they were agreed in proposing for this high office that tried friend and native of New England, Sir William Phipps.

I have been thus particular in showing the agency of Mr. Mather in procuring the provincial charter, because, in a civil point of view, this was, perhaps, the most important transaction of his life. Still, the procuring of the charter was not all that this indefatigable servant of the public accomplished, during his residence in England. He watched over the interests of *all* the New England colonies, endeavored to procure the restitution of their charters, and counteracted, so far as possible, the designs of their enemies. A design was on foot to unite the colony of Plymouth with New York. This was frustrated through the efforts of Mr. Mather, for which he received a letter of thanks from the general court of Plymouth.

In England, as every where else, Mr. Mather deeply interested himself in the concerns of religion. He was engaged in drawing up the well known "Heads of agreement between the Presbyterian and Congregational Churches" of England, and thus bringing about a closer union of these two separate bodies of Christians;—an object which would not, probably, have been accomplished, had it not been for his visit to that country. For the interest which he took in this matter, he received a vote of thanks from the General Assembly of Presbyterians in Devonshire, of which the celebrated John Flaval was moderator.

Meanwhile, he was doing all in his power to promote the interests of Harvard College. He presented its claims before the king, and solicited for it the patronage of nobles, and of other wealthy individuals. He was instrumental, if not of first turning the thoughts of Mr. Hollis towards the college, at least of encouraging and confirming him in his design of making it the object of his bounty.

It should be added, that during the four years Mr. Mather remained in England, he served his country gratis. "I never demanded," says he, "the least farthing as a recompense for the time I spent; and I procured donations to the province and the college, at least nine hundred pounds more than all the expenses of my agency came to."

Having, with much labor, secured for his native State a charter of government, (the best that could be secured) and having been honored with the nomination of the Governor, Lieutenant Governor, and the first Board of Council, who were to be appointed by the king, Mr. Mather left England, in company with the new Governor Phipps, in March, 1692, and arrived at Boston about the middle of May. The General Assembly was soon after convened, when "the Speaker, in the name of the House of Representatives, returned him thanks, for his faithful, painful, indefatigable endeavors to serve the country." The House also "appointed a day of solemn thanksgiving to Almighty God through the province, for granting a safe return to his excellency, the Governor, and the Rev. Increase Mather, who have industriously endeavored the service of this people, and brought over with them a settlement of government, in which their Majesties have graciously given us distinguishing marks of their royal favor and goodness."

It is not to be disguised, however, that there was a pretty strong party in the province, who were dissatisfied with the results of Mr. Mather's agency, and with him for his instrumentality in procuring them. Indeed, it had been the custom of the colonists, or of a portion of them, from the first, to find fault with their agents to England. The agent not being able to accomplish all that the people expected or desired, the fault was laid at his own door. The grounds of the dissatisfaction with Mr. Mather's proceedings were various. Some in what had been the Plymouth colony were dissatisfied, because they were now united with Massachusetts. Some were dissatisfied, that in his nominations to office, their names had been omitted; showing that human nature at that period, was not essentially different from what it is now. But the principal ground of dissatisfaction was the charter itself. It was not the *old* charter, which had been taken away; and then it contained some restrictions on what were conceived to be popular rights, which, by the former charter were secured; particularly, the right of electing some of the higher officers of government from among themselves.

It admits not of a doubt, however, at the present day, that Mr. Mather acted wisely, in this most important business. The restoration of the former charter could not be obtained; and if it could, without important modifications, it would not have been adapted to the altered and enlarged state of the colony. And had the agents returned without a charter, the way had been open for some second Andros to come and plunder, and distress the country.

Mr. Mather assumed, indeed, a high responsibility, in consenting to act in so important a matter without the concurrence of his colleagues; but the more credit is due to him on this account, and it belongs to posterity to award him this credit. It is impossible to conceive what New England might have been called to suffer,—what had been the fate of its churches, its schools, and its free institutions, had not the venerable Mather, with a far-sighted wisdom, and an unblanching firmness, seized the favorable opportunity, and accepted the charter which King William offered him. By this act, he lost somewhat of his former popularity, and exposed himself to no little reproach from a class of men—such as will be found, more or less, in every free country,—who prefer to find fault with the doings of others, rather than to incur responsibility themselves, and are fond of haranguing, about popular privileges and rights; but he met the decided approbation of the wise and good among his cotemporaries; while historians of a later date, and some who have not been disposed to mete out to him any thing more than even justice, have strongly approved of his conduct in this matter.

The following extract of a letter to the General Court at Boston, signed by twelve of the dissenting ministers of London, among whom were William Bates, John Howe, Samuel Annesly, and Isaac Chancy, will show how the conduct of Mr. Mather was regarded at the time, on the other side of the water. "Some among you may wonder that there has been so long delay, before your charter was finished; but if you consider the torrent of affairs in court, since the late revolution, it will lessen the wonder. The truth is, your affairs were so difficult and thorny, that the rare union of the wisdom of the serpent, and the innocence of the dove, was requisite, in the commissioners managing of them. A peremptory refusal of any charter, but of an uniform tenor with the first, had been like too strong a medicine, which exasperates the disease, instead of curing it. In affairs of great importance, it is wisdom maturely to deliberate, and consider conditional events, and by the foresight of inconveniences that will otherwise follow, to accept of such things as are best, in all their circumstances.

"We must, therefore, give this true testimony of our much esteemed and beloved brother, Mr. Increase Mather, that *with inviolate integrity excellent prudence, and unfainting diligence, he hath managed the great business committed to his trust.* As he is instructed in the school of heaven to minister in the affairs of the soul, so he is furnished with a talent to transact affairs of state. His proceedings have been with that caution and circumspection which is correspondent to the weight of his commission. He, with courage and constancy, has pursued the noble scope of his employment; and understanding the true moment of things, has preferred the public good to the vain conceits of some, that more might have been obtained, if peremptorily insisted on.

"Considering the open opposition and secret arts that have been used to frustrate the best endeavors for the interest of New England, the happy issue of these things is superior to our expectations. Your present charter secures liberty and property, the fairest flowers of the civil state; and what is incomparably more valuable, it secures the enjoyment of the blessed gospel, in its purity and freedom. Although there is a restraint of your power in some things that were granted in your former charter, yet there are more ample privileges in other things that may be of perpetual advantage to the colony.

"We doubt not your faithful agent will receive a gracious reward from above; and we hope his successful service will be welcomed with your entire approbation and grateful acceptance. We now, with ardent affection, recommend our dear brother to the Divine mercy, that through such dangerous seas he may safely arrive at his desired place. And we earnestly pray that the blessing of Heaven may be always upon your colony; that by the light and power of the gospel, the prince of darkness may be expelled from his ancient dominions, and the kingdom of our Saviour may be established and enlarged, by the accession of the American heathen to be his inheritance." Thus far the London Dissenting ministers, who at that period felt an interest in New England almost as great as though they had been members of the colony.

President Quincy, in his late history of Harvard University, thus speaks of the efforts of

Mr. Mather, on this occasion. "Whatever opinions we may be compelled to entertain concerning his measures and motives at other times, his conduct, in this great crisis of his country, entitles him to unqualified approbation. It is scarcely possible for a public agent to be placed in circumstances more trying and critical, nor could any one have exhibited more sagacity and devotedness to the true interests of his constituents. By his wisdom and firmness in acceding to the new charter, and thus assuming a responsibility of the weightiest kind, in opposition to his colleagues in the agency, he saved his country, apparently, from a rebellion, or a revolution, or from having a constitution imposed by the will of the transatlantic sovereign, and possibly at the point of the bayonet."—(Vol. I, p. 123.)

While Mr. Mather was abroad, he rarely omitted preaching on the Sabbath; for which he would accept no compensation, other than to engage the ministers to perform good offices for his country. He was particularly attached to the celebrated Dr. Bates of Hackney, for whom he preached regularly once a month, and with whose church he statedly partook of the Lord's supper.

He became intimately acquainted, also, with Mr. Baxter, now an old man, and had the satisfaction to visit him on his death-bed. In proof of the estimation in which he was held by Mr. Baxter, it may be mentioned, that this venerable man dedicated to him one of his latest publications, and in generous confidence made this request of him: "If, sir, you find errors in any of my writings, I charge you to confute them, after I am dead."

During Mr. Mather's absence from Boston, his ministerial duties were faithfully discharged by his son and colleague, Cotton Mather. At the same time, the college, of which he was president, was committed to the care and instruction of Mr. John Leverett, and Mr. William Brattle, tutors.

CHAPTER VIII.

Mr. Mather writes on the subject of Witchcraft. Opposes innovations in church order. His exertions for Harvard College. His connection with it dissolved. His character as President. Farewell address to the students.

Mr. Mather and Governor Phipps arrived in this country, in the midst of the famous excitement respecting witchcraft. The delusion had now been in progress several months, many were suffering from the supposed witches, while other many had been accused and imprisoned as the authors of the mischief. One of the first acts of the new governor was to institute a court for the trial of the accused; and one of the first acts of Mr. Mather was to write a book, with a view to allay the excitement, to expose false tests of innocence or guilt, and to refute a kind of *spectral evidence*, on which many were likely to be put to death. I shall have occasion to refer to Mr. Mather's agency in this matter, in another place. Suffice it to say here, that the publication which he issued was eminently seasonable, and was followed with the best results.

Upon the appearance of it, says his son, "the governor pardoned such as had been condemned, the confessors came, as it were, out of a dream wherein they had been fascinated, and many of the afflicted grew easy."

Mr. Mather was a strenuous supporter of the established faith and order of the New England churches; and when innovations were at any time attempted, they met from him a determined resistance. Near the close of the seventeenth century, an attempt was made to do away with the established practice of requiring of persons admitted to the Lord's table a particular account of their religious experience. The Rev. William Brattle, of Cambridge, was one of the promoters of this innovation. It was followed in a little time by the doctrine, openly promulgated by Mr. Stoddard and others, that *evidence of regeneration* is not to be required of candidates for the holy supper. This, Mr. Mather regarded as a very dangerous error, and opposed to it the whole weight of his influence and exertions. He wrote a preface to his son's life of Mitchell, in which he not only says, but proves by a variety of argument, that "doctrinal knowledge and outward blamelessness are *not* sufficient qualifications for admission to the church; but that practical confessions, or some relation of the work of conversion, are necessary." He would not have churches shut themselves up to this or that particular manner of obtaining satisfaction. It may be done orally, or in writing. It may be done by question and answer, or by a continuous narrative. But satisfaction should, in some way, be obtained. "Churches are bound in duty to inquire, not only into the knowledge and orthodoxy, but into the *spiritual estate* of those whom they receive to full communion in all the ordinances of Christ." At a later period, Mr. Mather engaged in controversy with Mr. Stoddard* on the terms of communion, or of admission to the church of Christ, showing, with great clearness and force, the unscriptural character of the views he advocated, and their dangerous bearing on the churches of New England.

Time has abundantly verified the correctness of Mr. Mather's conclusions, in relation to this subject. The doctrine and practice of Mr. Stoddard prevailed extensively for a season, till they were encountered and refuted, a hundred years ago, by his successor and grandson, President Edwards. The churches which then adopted the Edwardean views, or (which is the same,) came back to the ground of the early fathers of New England, together with those

* Mr. Stoddard, it will be recollected, was Mr. Mather's brother-in-law, having married his brother Eleazer's widow. See chap. I.

which have since sprung out of them, constitute in general, the Orthodox Congregational churches of the present day; while those which persisted in the Stoddardean views, became, with few exceptions, first Arminian, and then Unitarian.

About the same time with the controversy respecting terms of communion, another innovation was attempted, if indeed it be another, at which Mr. Mather was greatly troubled. It was the abandonment, by particular churches, of their separate, independent action, in the choice of their pastors, and their consenting to vote only in connection with the congregations. In the year 1697, the church of which Mr. Mather was pastor, sent "a letter of admonition to the church in Charlestown, for betraying the liberties of the churches, by putting into the hands of the whole inhabitants, the choice of a minister." The same year, measures were taken for founding the church in Brattle square, Boston, expressly excluding the distinct action of the church in the choice of a minister, and disclaiming "the requisition of any public relation of experiences, or any other examination than by the pastor," as the condition of being admitted to the Lord's supper. The Rev. Benjamin Colman, then a young man, and in England, was invited to become the first pastor of this church; and so confident were those who invited him, that he could not be ordained over it in this country, that they advised him to obtain ordination in England.

The leaders in this innovation, were Thomas Brattle, Esq., of Boston, Rev. William Brattle, of Cambridge, and Hon. John Leverett, afterwards president of Harvard College. I am the more particular in mentioning names, because I shall have occasion to refer to them again. The transaction was one which not only interested the feelings, and distressed the heart of Mr. Mather at the time, but it materially affected his situation afterwards. At the request and through the mediation of neighboring ministers and others, the members of the new church consented to modify very considerably their original plan, so that Mr. Mather met with them at the dedication of their house of worship, and even consented to preach on the occasion. Still, he was not satisfied with their proceedings, and he took occasion to express his dissatisfaction, in a treatise, published in the year 1700, entitled, "The Order of the Gospel professed by the Churches of New England, Justified." This gave rise to a reply, and that to a rejoinder, in which more heat and bitterness were manifested on both sides, than comport with our notions of clerical decency and propriety.

Mr. Mather, however, was not alone in his anxieties, at this time. Others besides him were induced to speak out, and to utter a solemn note of warning to those who were bent upon departing from the established customs of the churches. It was at this time, that the venerable Higginson, of Salem, and Hubbard, of Ipswich, published their joint "Testimony to the order of the Gospel in the Churches of New England,"—in which they say: "If any who are given to change, do rise up, to unhinge the well-established order of the churches in this land, it will be the duty and interest of the churches to examine, whether the men of this trespass are more prayerful, more watchful, more zealous, more patient, more heavenly, more universally conscientious, and harder students, and better scholars, and more willing to be informed and advised, than those great and good men who left unto the churches what they now enjoy. If they be not so, it will be wisdom for the children to forbear pulling down, with their own hands, the houses of God which were built by their wiser fathers, until they have better satisfaction. It is not yet forgotten by some surviving ear-witnesses, that when the Synod had finished the Platform of Church Discipline, (A. D. 1648,) they did, with an extraordinary elevation of soul and voice, then sing together *The song of Moses, the servant of God, and the song of the Lamb*, in the fifteenth chapter of the Revelations. God forbid, that in the loss of that holy discipline, there should hereafter be occasion to sing about breaking down the carved work of the house of God with axes and hammers, or to take up the eightieth Psalm for our lamentation."

Although the controversy here referred to, so far subsided, as to occasion no palpable breach of fellowship between those concerned in it, still, a degree of coldness and distance was observable, and they seem to have been the objects of mutual suspicion and jealousy, during the greater part of their lives.* This was the more unhappy for Mr. Mather, because those whose measures he had felt constrained to oppose, were the men chiefly concerned, at least for a time, in the direction and government of Harvard College.

The same year in which Mr. Mather returned

* This controversy, it will be recollected, was not about doctrines, but related only to questions of ecclesiastical order and discipline. Dr. Eliot tells us, that "the friendship between Dr. Colman and Cotton Mather, was renewed, several years before the latter died, and then they wondered how they had disagreed so long."

from England, (1692,) he prepared a charter for the college, which received the approbation of the governor, and the sanction of the general court. It was afterwards vetoed by the king; but while it continued in force, and the corporation had authority, under it, to confer honorary degrees, they conferred on him the degree of Doctor of Divinity. It is remarkable, that this degree had never before been conferred in British America; nor was it conferred again, until almost eighty years afterwards, it was bestowed on the Rev. Samuel Mather, (grandson of Increase,) and on the Rev. Nathaniel Appleton, of Cambridge.

Repeated attempts were made, during the next seven or eight years, to procure a charter for the college, which should receive the sanction of the king; and in more than one instance, President Mather seemed on the point of embarking for England, with a view to the furtherance of this important object. But for one cause or another, all these attempts failed, and the college continued in an unsettled and embarrassed state.

During the troubles of this period, President Mather proposed repeatedly to resign his office; but the proposition was discouraged and resisted by the corporation. It was an object with the

General Court to induce him to resign his pastoral charge, and reside at Cambridge; but he could not be satisfied that this was his duty. To gratify the friends of the college, he did remove to Cambridge for a few months; but neither he nor his family seem to have been happy, nor were his people willing that he should be taken from them. Consequently, he soon returned to Boston.

It was this question of residence, which finally closed his connection with the college. He seems not properly to have *resigned* his office, but on his refusing to reside at Cambridge, the duties of it passed out of his hands,* and devolved on those of Rev. Samuel Willard, who was appointed vice-president.

That Dr. Mather was faithful and successful in the office of President, notwithstanding the many disadvantages under which the office was sustained, is testified by all who have written on the subject. Mr. Peirce, in his valuable history of Harvard University, says: "Dr. Mather's services at the college were assiduous and faithful. The moral and religious instruction

* The general assembly passed a vote, that *no man should act as President of the college, who did not reside at Cambridge.* Mr. Mather did not think it his duty to reside there. Consequently, his connection with the college ceased.

of the students had his particular attention. The college appears to have been in a flourishing condition, while he was at its head. Its numbers increased, and it was enriched, in no small degree, by the hand of munificence." Page 64.

President Quincy also says: "That Dr. Mather was well qualified for the office of President, and had conducted himself in it faithfully and laboriously, is attested by the history of the college, the language of the legislature, and the acknowledgment of his cotemporaries." Vol. I. p. 116.

He was vigilant and faithful in the *government* of college, requiring a strict conformity to wholesome laws, and firmly resisting all attempts at insubordination. He was particularly concerned for the *spiritual* welfare of his pupils. He preached to them every week, often expounded to them the Scriptures, advised them as to what books they should read, and cautioned them against such as he considered hurtful. He used frequently to send for them into the library, and there pray and converse with them separately, warning them of the terrible consequences of continued impenitence, and charging them to turn from their sins and live. Not a few of them, we are assured, "will bless God all their days for these admonitions, and will never forget the words that quickened them."

In June, 1701, Dr. Mather preached a farewell sermon to his pupils, from Colossians 3: 11. "*Christ is all, and in all.*" In the conclusion of his discourse, he thus addressed them: "Unto you that are students in the college, and more especially unto such of you as are (what most of you are) designed for the work of the ministry, the advice which I now leave is this:

"1. Let the *glorifying of the Lord Jesus Christ*, and not any worldly considerations, induce you to devote yourselves to the evangelical ministry. True, it is an honorable calling upon which you are entering. To be ambassadors of the King of kings, is to be in an honorable station. But you must not propose the *honors* of this world, in what you undertake. No, but expect rather to be despised and rejected of men, and to have all manner of indignities heaped upon you. As little may you propose the *riches* of this world. The low and mean intention of *getting a living* must not be the chief thing in your eye. You may, no doubt, gain much more wealth, by betaking yourselves to some other employments; while in that of the ministry, poverty, narrow and humbling circumstances, and grievous defraudations from an unthankful people, are what you may look for. You must count it honor enough, and riches enough, if Christ may have service from you. The *special advantages to serve Christ*, which ministers have above other men,—let these be the honor and the riches on which your hearts are mainly set.

"2. Let your sermons be *full of Christ*. Sermons full of *self*, and made for the ostentation of your own learning; are these the sacrifices with which God is well pleased? The sermons of the Apostles were not such. No; they could say, 'We preach not ourselves, but *Christ Jesus the Lord*.' Paul 'preached those things which concern *the Lord Jesus Christ*.' Alas, there are preachers in this world, who have little of Christ in their sermons. A morality, without the gospel of Christ—nothing higher than what may be met with in a Cicero, a Seneca, an Epictetus, a Plutarch, is to be found there. They would think it a disparagement unto their sermons to have the name of Christ often mentioned in them. How unlike are such to that pattern preacher, who has the name of Christ no less than ten times, in the ten first verses of his first Epistle to the Corinthians? There is matter enough in the very name Christ, to be the subject of your meditation, all your days.

Do not then neglect to preach on the glories, the person, the offices, the actions, and the benefits of Christ, and of the interest he has in every article of our religion. Know the truth, as it is *in Jesus*. Hence,

"3. Have an eye still to Christ, when you are preaching on other subjects. Other subjects are to be preached upon; but Christ is to be the end and the aim of all. The evil of sin is to be preached upon, and so is the misery of man fallen by sin; but it must be to lead your hearers unto Christ, who alone is mighty to save. The moral law is to be preached upon, as the rule of our obedience; and so are the duties of piety, equity, and charity. But the example of Christ, obeying the law, and a leaning upon him for assistance and acceptance in all we do, is always to accompany these subjects. Remember, that the *life* of your preaching will be in proportion to what there is of Christ, who is *the Life*, shining through it.

"If, my beloved pupils, you do thus glorify Christ, God, even his eternal Father, will glorify you. For there is nothing so dear to him, as the Son of his love. Christ is dearer to the Father, than all the men on the earth, and all the angels in heaven. Christ is dearer to him than all the worlds he has ever made ; since it is for him that he has made them all. God delights exceedingly to see Christ glorified ; and if this be what your hearts are set upon, he will reward you openly and abundantly. You will have this reward among the rest—*the Holy Spirit breathing powerfully in your ministry.* The Spirit of truth will *glorify me*, saith the Saviour. The blessed Spirit will sadly withdraw from a ministry that has not a Christ animating it. He will own and honor that ministry in which Christ is truly and faithfully preached.

"And now, my children, what shall I more say to you? I hope that, as to many of you (O that it might be all!) I shall meet you with joy at the right hand of Christ, in the great day of his appearing and kingdom. But if any of you prove so miserable as to die in your sins, and in a Christless condition, I protest unto you this day, that I shall testify against you before the Lord Jesus Christ, that I have called upon you, both publicly and privately, to make sure of an interest in him. I am pure, therefore, from the blood of your souls. If any of you (which may infinite mercy prevent,) shall die in your sins, your blood will be upon your own heads."

Thus were the students of Harvard College

addressed, by their President, almost one hundred and fifty years ago. Where shall we look for words more fitly spoken? When shall the members of that venerable seminary be addressed in like manner again?

CHAPTER IX.

Life of Dr. Mather subsequent to his resigning the Presidency. His habits as a student. His liberality. His gentlemanly manners. His character as a preacher. His solemn testimony. His humility and penitence. His last sickness, death, funeral, &c.

Dr. Mather's connection with the college ceased, as we have seen, A. D. 1701. After this he lived about twenty-two years, during the greater part of which time he performed his ministerial duties much as usual, and continued to take a watchful interest in every thing which concerned church and state. In this time also, and in addition to all his other labors, he issued from the press not far from fifty distinct publications, the most of them on important practical subjects.

I have said that, during this latter portion of his life, Dr. Mather exercised his ministry much as usual. When he had been settled forty-nine years, he preached a *Jubilee* sermon; and as the servants in Israel were released at the Jubilee, so he requested a release from any further public labors. But his people set too high a value on his services, to consent to such a proposition

At a later period, they kindly voted, that "the labors of the pulpit should be expected from him only when he found himself able and inclined to perform them." Still, he actually did preach frequently and powerfully, to the very last year of his life.

Dr. Mather was an indefatigable student, all his days. Indeed, prayer and study may be said to have constituted his principal business. His people sometimes complained that they saw so little of him in their families, and from the following account of the manner in which he ordinarily spent his time, we think their complaints were not without reason. "In the morning, repairing to his study, he deliberately read a chapter, and offered prayer, and then plied what of reading and writing he had before him. At nine o'clock he came down, read a chapter, and made a prayer with his family; after which he returned to the work of the study. Coming down to dinner, he quickly went up again, and commenced the afternoon with another prayer; when he went on with his studies till evening. The studies of the evening were commenced with another prayer, and went on till nine o'clock. Then he came down to his family sacrifices. From these, he again repaired to the study, where he continued, often, till after midnight. The studies of the day were always closed with prayer. Sixteen hours of the four and twenty were commonly spent after this manner in the study."

Not a few, on reading this account, will wonder how the subject of it lived to the long period of eighty-four years. Most ministers, with so little relaxation and exercise, would have died of dyspepsia or hypochondria, in one sixth part of the time. But if Dr. Mather *could live* and enjoy health, none need wonder at the interest which continued to be felt in his publications and pulpit performances. His intellectual machinery never grew rusty from disuse. He not only kept up with his age, but kept in advance of it. Younger men might study as hard, and preach as well as they could; he studied harder, and preached better. To all the advantages of intellectual progress and new discoveries and improvements, in respect to which he was on a par with them, he added the more important advantages of a long experience, which were beyond their reach. In this way, Dr. Mather continued to bear fruit in old age; and his example is one of great importance to ministers and others, as they approach the evening of life. Most old men lay off their armor, and retire from the duties of active life too soon. They conclude prematurely that their work is done, and their usefulness ended. There is no reason why clergymen, who enjoy good health, should not be better ministers, and more useful preachers, between the ages of fifty and seventy, than between those of thirty and fifty. Let them study, if not as closely as Dr. Mather, enough at least to be even with their age, and in advance of it; let them keep up their interest in the concerns of the church and world, and their habits of activity and usefulness; more especially, let them grow, as did the venerable man of whom we are speaking, in prayerfulness and heavenly mindedness; and there will be little danger of their becoming stale and neglected. They will, like him, bear fruit in old age, and their labors will be appreciated and blessed.

Dr. Mather, like most other ministers, was little burthened with this world's goods; but in the use of what he had, he was truly liberal. He was so, on strictly Christian principles. He believed that, as God has reserved a seventh part of our *time* to be devoted more especially to his service, so he has required a *tenth part* of our substance. Accordingly, he constantly devoted a tithe of his income to pious and charitable uses. This, he held, was *the least* which a

Christian could in conscience do. He often did much more than this.

That habit of prayerfulness and communion with God, in which Dr. Mather so uniformly lived, imparted to him, not sternness and severity of manner, but a remarkable *seriousness* and *gravity*. He lived, and he seemed to live, as seeing him who is invisible. His very presence was a rebuke and a check to every thing bordering upon indecency or levity.

Still, he was distinguished above most men of his age for *ease and gentleness of manner*, or for what may be denominated *true Christian courtesy*. It is required of a bishop, in the Scriptures, that he be "of *good behavior.*" Dr. Goodwin interprets this to mean, that he "must not be slovenly, nor of such an unmannerly carriage as to bring his calling into contempt. He must avoid all that rudeness that flows from ill nature, or ill nurture, and be of such a modest, comely, pleasing behavior as to render him fit for the company of gentlemen." Such, preeminently, was Dr. Mather. Recluse as he was at some periods, he had mingled much with the world at others. He had frequented the best company, both in this country and in Europe. It had been his lot to stand before kings. And it is testified of him that "he was of a very pleasing behavior, full of gravity, but exhibiting the carriage and neatness of a gentleman."

In point of learning, Dr. Mather exceeded all the New England fathers, with the single exception of Cotton Mather, his son. But though less learned than his son, and possessing less exuberance of fancy, he had more sound, practical judgment—more common sense. His publications many of them are still extant. The style will compare with that of the best authors of the seventeenth century.

As a preacher, Dr. Mather was at the head of his profession in this country. I question, indeed, whether he had many superiors in the English nation. His discourses were eminently *scriptural.* "God's word," he said, "is the food of souls, and the more there is of that pertinently introduced, the better fed will be the flock." His manner in preaching was elevated, often eloquent, yet always plain to the humblest capacity. "His aim was, not to shoot over the heads of his hearers, but into their hearts. He concealed every other art, that he might the better practice the one single art of being intelligible.

He used no notes in preaching, to the very last. He was not opposed to the use of notes, but only to the servile reading of them. "He would have more speaking, and less reading, in our sermons. He would have the preacher be so much of an orator, that the appropriate vigor and address of a sermon might not be lost."

In delivery, he was grave and deliberate, but not monotonous. He had a commanding voice, and he used it often with great effect. The emphatical clauses and sentences were delivered, says his son, "with such a *tonitruous cogency*, that the hearers were struck with awe, like that produced by the fall of thunderbolts."

I only add, that Dr. Mather's ministry was a *prayerful* one. He continually sought the Divine director in the choice of his subjects, and as to the manner in which he should treat them. He always went from his knees to the pulpit; and the first thing, on his return from the pulpit, was to give thanks for the assistance he had enjoyed, and ask a blessing on the truths he had delivered.

A few months before Dr. Mather's death, he prepared a written *testimony*, as to the design of the pilgrims in settling this country, and the obligations that were resting upon their descendants, to see this design carried out and consummated. "I am now," says he, "in the eighty fourth year of my age, and am every hour waiting and longing for my dismission to a better world. In these very solemn circumstances, I am willing to add my *testimony;* and I do hereby declare, that the *principal design* upon which these colonies were first planted, was to profess, and practice, and enjoy, with undisturbed liberty, *the holy religion of God our Saviour*, as exhibited in the sacred Scriptures, and rescued from the inventions and abuses which the man of sin has introduced; also, to set up *churches* for our Lord Jesus Christ, that shall keep themselves loyal to him, their glorious King, receiving his word as their only standard and law. It was equally designed by those followers of the Lord into this wilderness, that the pure and undefiled religion delivered unto us in the Scriptures, and exhibited afterwards in our confession of faith, should be continually preached, and the doctrines of grace particularly asserted, by ministers of good abilities, godliness, and watchfulness, freely and fairly chosen by the churches whereof they are the pastors. It belongs also to these churches to be so constituted, as manifestly to exhibit the kingdom of heaven unto the world, both debarring from their communion such ignorant and scandalous persons as are to be shut out from the city of God, and admitting all those (though of different persuasions about lesser points,) of whom it may be judged, that Christ has received them to the glory of God. *Our foundation is in these holy mountains.*

"It is now the dying wish of one that has been about three score and six years, after a poor manner, but I hope with some sincerity, serving the best of masters in the blessed work of the gospel, that *these churches may stand fast in the faith and order of the gospel, and hold fast what they have received, that no man take their crown;* and that the pastors would more distinctly, and with proper inculcations, from time to time, acquaint the churches with their true interest, and those things which will be for their beauty and safety. It is also my desire, as one who has sustained for many years the office of President, that the tutors in our colleges, from which the churches expect their supplies, would see to it that the students are well informed in those points which it most concerns them to know, that so the work of God among us may not be marred, by falling into unskillful and unfaithful hands.

"Indeed, I cannot but go the way of all the earth rejoicing, that the means which have been so indefatigably used for drawing away unwary people into the things that will not profit them, have hitherto had so little success; and that the body of the more sober people throughout the country continue to discover so strong an aversion to those things, from the face of which their fathers fled into this wilderness. But there may be danger of another generation rising up, which will not know the Lord, nor the works done by him and for him, among his people here. I therefore, from the suburbs of that glorious world into which I am now entering, do earnestly testify unto the rising generation, that if they sinfully forsake the God, the hope, and the religious ways of their pious ancestors, *the glorious Lord will severely punish their apostasy, and be terrible unto them from his holy places.*

"The Lord our God be with you, as he was with your fathers. Let him not leave you, nor forsake you. And now, Lord, let thy work appear unto thy servants, and thy glory unto their children, and *establish thou the work of our hands upon us ; yea, the work of our hands establish thou it.*"

It is a remarkable fact in the experience of good men, that the more they grow in knowledge and in grace, the more they grow in humility, in penitence, and in deep and affecting views of their own unworthiness. So it was with Job. "I have heard of thee by the hearing of the ear, but now mine eyes seeth thee; wherefore *I abhor myself, and repent in dust and ashes.*" So it was with Isaiah. "Woe is me, for I am undone; for *I am a man of unclean lips.*" So it was with the apostle Paul. "O wretched man that I am; who shall deliver me from the body of this death!" The experience of Dr. Mather was very similar to that here referred to. Though one of the most blameless of men in all his demeanor, so far as the eyes of others could follow him, yet through his whole life, and more especially in the latter part of it, we hear him complaining of his indwelling corruptions, and of his not keeping his thoughts and heart as he desired. In his diary, he constantly charges himself with remaining iniquities, unfruitfulness, pride, worldliness, and a great unmeetness for the service and the kingdom of God. "Alas, how unfruitful am I! How do I misspend my time! How do I ever cumber the ground!" His sins were "such a sorrow and burthen to him, that they exceedingly reconciled him to the dying hour, which he always spoke of with sensible transport, when that advantage of it came to be mentioned: *Never sin any more.*"

I have said that growing Christians are usually characterized by a growing sense of personal unworthiness. This fact may seem strange to some; still, it is one not hard to be accounted for. As the Christian learns more of the extent and purity of God's law, he discovers more of the number and magnitude of his transgressions. As he sees more clearly the beauty and excellency of holiness, he feels more deeply the defilement and the guilt of sin. He finds new sources of evil opening in his heart, and points of duty before unobserved, and of course neglected, rise up to view and require attention. And thus, while he is improving in all goodness, he seems to himself often to be deteriorating. He seems to remain at a vast and increasing distance from that point of perfection towards which he aims.

Dr. Mather's last sickness was a very distressing one, affecting the mind as well as the body. He had occasional seasons of darkness and depression,—the result, doubtless, of disease,—when doubts and fears obtruded themselves upon him, lest, peradventure, he should be deceived at the last. But in times of the greatest darkness, "he still discovered such a holy solicitude, that he might not in anything dishonor God, nor lose his hold of the blessed Jesus, nor break the resolution which he had made seventy years before, and on which he now looked back with unspeakable consolation, as was altogether to be preferred to those joys of impulse with which some, in their dying moments, are transported." It has been well determined by the best judges, "that going to heaven in the way of *repentance*, is much safer and surer than in the way of *extasy*."

Still, the pathway of Dr. Mather through the valley of the shadow of death was not all dark. Occasionally the clouds were scattered, and he was enabled to rejoice, in hope of the glory that was so soon to be revealed. He very often said, "The infinite mercy of God, and the infinite merit of Christ, keep me above all discouragement." These words of Christ were also a comfort to him: "Where I am, *there shall my servant be*." He delighted to read and ponder the seventy-first Psalm. "O God, thou hast taught me from my youth, and hitherto have I declared thy wondrous works. Now also, when I am old and gray-headed, O God, forsake me not. I will make mention of *thy righteousness*, even of *thine only*."

During his last sickness, Dr. Mather received a message from his excellent friend, Mr. Thomas Hollis of London, inquiring whether he were yet in the land of the living. To this he replied: "Tell him I am not in the land of the living, but am going to it. This poor world is the land of the dying. Heaven only is the true land of the living."

The last morning of his life, says Cotton Mather, "perceiving that his dying agonies were now upon him, I did what I could to strengthen him with such quickening words as the lively oracles have provided for such occasions. As it grew towards noon, I said to him: 'Sir, the messenger has now come to tell thee, "This day shalt thou be with me in Paradise." Do you believe it, sir, and rejoice in the views and the hopes of it?' He replied, '*O yes, I do! I do! I do!*' And with these words he died in my arms."

His death occurred August 23, 1723. His disease, like that of his father, was the stone, from which, for several successive weeks, he had suffered intensely. On the seventh day after his death, he was interred, with all the honors due to his character, and to the rank he had so long held in society. Governor Dummer, Chief Justice Sewall, President Leverett, and three of the principal ministers, bore the pall. Not less than fifty ministers, one hundred and sixty students and alumni of college, and a train of citizens and spectators that could not be numbered, followed him to his grave. The funeral sermon was preached by Rev. Mr. Foxcroft, one of the pastors of the first church, from 2 Chron. 24: 15, 16, "He was full of days, when he died; . . . . . and they buried him in the city of David, among the kings, because he had done good in Israel, both towards God and towards his house."

Dr. Mather was eighty-four years old when he died. He had been a preacher sixty-six years, during almost sixty of which he was pastor of the Old North Church in Boston. Dr. Eliot speaks of him as "the *father* of the New England clergy, whose name and character were held in veneration, not only by those who knew him, but by succeeding generations." For many years before his death, he was commonly spoken of as "the Patriarch," and "the Jehoiada of New England."

About twenty years before his death, Dr. Mather had a controversy, as we have before seen, on questions of church order and discipline, which gave him much uneasiness at the time, and led to painful forebodings as to the prospect of New England. But these difficulties at length subsided, and the evils resulting from them—owing in great measure, no doubt, to his resistance—were far less extensive than he feared. The churches and ministers of Boston seemed inclined to rally round the Platform, and cling to the established usages of New England. This was a great consolation to the venerable Mather, in his last days. "He left the world rejoicing, that the glorious Lord had seen fit to entrust his churches here to such pious, painful, and every way desirable hands. He saw a class of young ministers introduced into the city, whom he esteemed more precious than so many golden wedges of Ophir. When he saw given to the churches a Sewall, a Prince, a Webb, a Cooper, a Foxcroft, a Waldron, all singularly endeared to him, and saw others of a like character coming on after them, it is inexpressible with what joy he regarded them, and with what earnestness he entreated them to walk in the truth, and to plead for it."

CHAPTER X.

Increase Mather vindicated, from the charge of promoting witchcraft. From the charge of injuriously treating the founders of the Brattle Street Church. From the charge of injuring Gov. Dudley. From the charge of being the dupe of his own impressions. From the imputation of selfish and ambitious motives. From the general, wholesale charges of President Quincy, and others.

For the first century after Dr. Mather's death, his character and reputation were unassailed and untarnished. They were suffered to remain, much as he had left them, in the hands of his immediate survivors. But within the last few years, certain writers in and around Boston, who have no sympathy with the religion of the Mathers, have undertaken to revile and defame him. With Cotton Mather I have at present nothing to do, except so far as his acts and character are identified with those of his father. But in a life of Increase Mather, it would be unpardonable not to inquire into the correctness of some of the principal charges which have been urged against him.

He has been charged, in the first place, with

an effective instrumentality in *producing* and *prolonging* the excitement in New England respecting witchcraft. "That both the Mathers," says President Quincy, "had an efficient agency in producing and prolonging that excitement, there can be, at this day, no possible question."*

How Increase Mather could have had any agency in *producing* the excitement here referred to, it is hard to conceive. The strange appearances at Salem village, (now Danvers,) commenced in February, 1692, when Dr. Mather was in England, where he had constantly resided, and where he had been most intensely occupied with the important duties of his agency for nearly four years. How then could he have been instrumental in *producing* this excitement?

And the charge of *prolonging* it is even more unfounded than that of producing it. He arrived at home May 14, 1692, when the excitement was at its highest point. Shortly afterwards, as soon as it could possibly be prepared, he published his treatise, entitled "Cases of Conscience respecting Witchcraft," in which, "with incomparable reason and reading," he refuted the received doctrine of *spectral evidence*, on the ground of which so many innocent per-

* History of Harvard University, vol. I, p. 62.

sons had been tried and condemned. Immediately upon this, says Cotton Mather, the governor "pardoned such as had been condemned," and the accused were, I believe, in all cases acquitted. "The confessors, too, came as it were out of a dream, wherein they had been fascinated, and the afflicted, in most instances, grew easy." It would seem from this account, given by an eye witness, that instead of contributing to prolong the excitement, Dr. Mather was a principal instrument in bringing it to a close.

That he was a believer in witchcraft, there can be no doubt; as who in that age, whether learned or unlearned, physicians, ministers, or lawyers, were not? Such was the common faith of Christendom, and had been so for hundreds of years. Persons who have not attended particularly to the subject can have no idea of the extent to which the supposed crime of witchcraft has prevailed in different countries, and the multitude of deaths which it has occasioned. In the latter part of the sixteenth century, not only hundreds but thousands were put to death—many of them by the extremest tortures—in different parts of Europe, under the imputation of witchcraft. In the year 1664, Sir Matthew Hale presided at the trial of two females in Suffolk, supposed to be witches, both of whom were condemned and executed. A few years later, many were tried and condemned in England, under the administration of Chief Justice Holt. The last execution for witchcraft in England was at Huntingdon, in the year 1716; and the last in Scotland was at Dornoch, Sutherlandshire, in 1722. The English statute against witchcraft, making it a capital offence, was not repealed, until the year 1736. Sir William Blackstone, the great oracle of British law, who died no longer ago than 1780, declared his belief in witchcraft in the following terms; "To deny the possibility, nay the *actual existence* of witchcraft and sorcery, is at once flatly to contradict the revealed word of God, in various passages both of the Old and New Testaments; and the thing itself is a truth to which every nation in the world hath, in its turn, borne testimony, either by examples seemingly well attested, or by prohibitory laws, which suppose at least the possibility of commerce with evil spirits."

In New England, at the time of Increase Mather, the belief in witchcraft may be said to have been universal. The most experienced physicians who were called to prescribe for the sufferers, and the most eminent ministers who were invited to pray with them, did not hesitate to pronounce them bewitched. Even those persons who had the least sympathy with the Mathers on some subjects, as Thomas and William Brattle, John Leverett, and Robert Calef, all agreed with them as to the *reality* of witchcraft. Thomas Brattle wrote a book in opposition to the proceedings of the times, in which he holds that, not only the afflicted, but most of the confessors "were *possessed with the devil*, and therefore not fit to be regarded, as to anything they say of themselves or others." There can be no doubt that Increase Mather adopted the current belief of the times as to the reality and the sin of witchcraft. But that he had any instrumentality in prodûcing or prolonging the excitement in New England on that subject, as alleged by President Quincy, is an entirely groundless accusation. Indeed, he is expressly mentioned by Mr. Brattle, as one of those who "utterly condemned" the proceedings of the courts, affirming that, if persisted in, they would "ruin and undo poor New England."

Another charge, or rather series of charges against Dr. Mather, has grown out of his treatment of the Messrs. Brattle, Leverett, Colman, and others, in reference to the founding of the Brattle Street Church. He is represented as acting, in this instance, under the influence of "excited temper and wounded pride;" as exhibiting "great violence and personality, an ill-governed and overbearing spirit." He was roused "to such a height of indignation, as to lose all sense of prudence and character, all patience and self-possession."* But after much attention to the subject, I can see no sufficient grounds for these heavy, wholesale accusations. That Dr. Mather was conscientiously attached to the order of the New England churches, as established by the Cambridge Platform, and was disposed to discountenance any considerable departures from it, there can be no doubt. That he was especially dissatisfied with those alarming innovations which the Brattles and Mr. Leverett were laboring to introduce, is equally clear.† He would be led, therefore, not by "excited temper or wounded pride," but by the dictates of his *conscience*, and *the fear of God*, to oppose these innovations, and to discountenance the men who

* Quincy's History, Vol. I. pp. 133—143.

† "These men," says President Quincy, "refused to inquire into the regeneration of communicants; denied the necessity of explicit covenanting with God and the church; admitted that persons not communicants might elect pastors; referred admission to the sacraments to the prudence and conscience of the minister; and held that admission to the pastoral relation might be valid, without the approbation of neighboring churches." Vol. I, p. 200. Now whatever President Quincy may think of these innovations, Dr. Mather certainly deemed them of most alarming import. He saw that, if they were not discountenanced, these churches of New England, this "garden of the Lord," as our fathers termed it, would be undone.

insisted on promoting them. He would labor by all fair means—and I have yet to learn that he used any other—to counteract the example and influence of these men, so far as their objectionable measures were concerned, and to keep the college from falling into their hands.

This was one cause, I have no doubt, which led President Mather, near the close of his connection with the college, to hesitate as to the duty of resigning his office. He had before wished, and repeatedly proposed to resign; but he now seemed rather to shrink from it, well knowing into whose hands the institution was likely to fall. He could not think it right to leave his flock in Boston, and become a resident at Cambridge, but was willing to discharge the office of President, as he had long done to general acceptance; and if the legislature would not consent to this, he preferred that they, not he, should take the responsibility of closing his connection with the college.

As little can it be doubted, that those who differed from him on questions of church order were exerting, at this time, a secret influence to get the college out of his hands, hoping and expecting that it might fall into their own. It was owing in great measure to their influence, that the legislature pursued the course it did. As

Cotton Mather tells the story, his enemies "obtained a vote, that no man should act as President of the college, who did not reside at Cambridge;" well knowing "that Dr. Mather would not remove his habitation from a loving people at Boston, to reside at Cambridge, while the college was as it then was," i. e. without a charter, and consequently in an unsettled, embarrassed state; "and that in this way they should get the college out of his hands. It should be borne in mind, that Mr. Leverett was, at this time, a leading member, and I believe the speaker, of the House of Representatives.

I will not say that in Dr. Mather's controversial publications, growing out of what he honestly conceived to be the irregular constitution of the Brattle street church, there are no expressions which we may think unwarrantably severe. But thus much may at least be said: the controversy was conducted with more decency on his part, than on the other; and the severe expressions on both sides are to be attributed more, probably, to the fashion of the age, than to the spirit and character of the men. And as one very justly remarks, "It is unfair to take a man out of his own age, and try him by the standard of another."

It must be said also, in relation to this whole

controversy, that the points for which Dr. Mather contended, though not strictly points of doctrine, are yet of a vitally important character. So he regarded them; and so they are regarded by evangelical Christians at the present day. He saw that if the principles of Stoddard, and the Brattles, and Leverett, and some others, in regard to the admission of persons to the church, were generally adopted, the churches would ere long be filled up with unconverted members, and the pulpits with unconverted ministers, and that the vital power of the gospel, if not its most essential truths, would be lost sight of and discarded. He saw that if the churches gave up the primitive inestimable right of electing, independently, their own ministers, very soon they would have ministers placed over them, from whose unholy influence they must either flee away, or under it they must consent to remain and be corrupted.

The experience of almost a century and a half has shown that Dr. Mather's conclusions and forebodings were well founded. With regard to many of the Pilgrim churches, the worst that he feared from the mistakes of his cotemporaries has been more than realized. And that the desolations resulting, in part, from the innovations then made, had not an earlier and a wider spread, is owing, in great measure, to the resistance which he opposed to them; so that now, after the lapse of five generations, we may look back upon Increase Mather as the man who, in the face of much obloquy and personal sacrifice, not only gave to Massachusetts a constitution of government, but saved the great body of her churches from a tide of ruin, which was beginning to set in, and threatening to roll over them.

Another of the objections to Dr. Mather relates to his treatment of Governor Dudley. On the 12th of September, 1707, Vice President Willard died; and in the month following, John Leverett was elected President of Harvard College. There can be no doubt that the election was displeasing to Dr. Mather. It is now pretended that he expected himself to be restored to the presidency, or at least that the office would have been given to his son; and that he was so angry with Governor Dudley for defeating his own, or his son's appointment, and favoring the election of Mr. Leverett, that he immediately addressed to the Governor a letter, "breathing a spirit of abuse and virulence, of which the records of party animosity contain but few parallels." *

* Quincy's History Vol. I., p. 201.

With respect to this letter to Governor Dudley, I remark, in the first place, that if President Quincy's dates are correct, (which there is some reason to doubt) the letter was written months before the death of Vice President Willard, or the election of Leverett, and of course could not have been prompted by any feelings which the writer entertained growing out of that event. The date of the letter, as given by President Quincy, is "20th of January, 1707;" whereas Willard died in the September following, and Leverett was elected in October.

But whatever may be thought as to the correctness of dates, I remark, secondly, there is not in this letter of Dr. Mather, a single word, or the remotest allusion, respecting any expectations of the writer as to the presidency, either for himself, or for his son. Neither does it contain the slightest allusion to the election of Mr. Leverett, or to any influence which the Governor may be supposed to have exerted in favor of that event. Indeed, the letter contains but a single reference to the College in any way; and that, as we shall see, is quite distinct and remote from the subject of the presidency.

But not to dwell on preliminaries, let us come to the letter itself. And in order to understand the full purport of it, it will be necessary that we know something of the history and character of Governor Dudley. He was the son of Thomas Dudley, one of the first settlers and Governors of the Massachusetts colony, and was graduated at Harvard College in 1665. In his youth, he seemed to be truly religious, and used to speak of Dr. Mather as his "spiritual father." He was educated for the Christian ministry, and was once talked of as colleague with Dr. Mather in Boston. He soon engaged, however, in civil pursuits, after which his religious impressions seem to have presented no obstacle in the way of his ambition. He was in high favor with the oppressors of the colony, at the time when the charter was taken away. He was the first officer in the government, before Andros arrived. Under him, he was president of the council, and chief justice, and was deeply concerned in all the oppressions of those troublous times. In the subsequent revolution, when Andros and his creatures were imprisoned, Dudley was kept in close confinement, and was treated even more harshly than any of them, as being thought more inexcusably guilty. Had it not been for the interposition of Cotton Mather (for Increase was then in England), he would probably have been torn in pieces by the violence of the mob. He was ordered to England to give an account of himself, in 1689, and the next year he was made Chief Justice of New York.

While Sir William Phipps was governor of Massachusetts, Dudley exerted all his influence and cunning to injure him, hoping to succeed him in the government, if by any means it could be got out of his hands. During the short administration of Lord Bellamont, he was intriguing to secure favor, in both Old England and New, that if possible he might be again seated in the chair of his native state. He had always professed a great regard for the Mathers; when in Boston, he attended frequently if not statedly, on their ministry;* and he had now the address to procure a letter from Cotton Mather to king William, which had much influence in his favor. He was appointed governor of Massachusetts in the year 1702, in which situation he continued during the next fourteen years. "The first seven years," says Eliot, "were spent in debates with the House of Representatives, or in private disputes with men who ceased not to accuse him of artifice and deception, of arbitrary conduct, and of enmity even

* In a letter to Increase Mather, dated May 17, 1686, Dudley says: "For the things of *my soul,* I have these many years hung upon your lips, and ever shall; and in *civil things,* I am desirous you may know, with all plainness, my reasons of procedure, and that they may be satisfactory to you."

to those privileges which they had obtained by the new charter." It was near the close of these first seven years that Dr. Mather, considering the relations which had subsisted between himself and the governor, and the favors which he had conferred upon him, and being wearied and disgusted with the course of his administration, addressed to him the letter of which we speak. It is a plain, searching and faithful letter, such as few governors of Dudley's character ever received, and for which he had much more reason to be grateful, than to be angry. It is too long to be published entire, in these pages. A brief abstract of it is all that I can at present offer.*

In the first place, Dr. Mather expresses his fears that the governor had been guilty of receiving bribes. And he mentions several instances of this nature, which had been *sworn to* by some of the most respectable men in the province.

Next, he tells the governor of his fears, that "he had been contriving to destroy the charter privileges of the province," and introduce another government like that of Andros. And Mr. Bancroft, in his History of the United

* The letter may be found entire in the Massachusetts Historical Collections, Series 1., Vol. III., p. 126. Cotton Mather wrote the governor a letter at the same time.

States, assures us that this was true. He says expressly that "Governor Dudley, and for a season his son also, became the active opponents of the chartered liberties of New England, endeavoring to effect their overthrow, and the establishment of a general government, as in the days of Andros.*

In the third place, Dr. Mather expresses to the governor his fears, that he had been hypocritical, and inconsistent in respect to the college; particularly (if I understand him) in his attempts to revive, by mere provincial authority, the old college charter of 1650, which he had often before represented to be dead, and never to be revived but by the assent of the king. And President Quincy is of the same opinion with Dr. Mather, on this subject. He represents this act of Dudley, in reviving the old college charter, without the assent of the king, as "irreconcilable with the duties growing out of the rela-

* Vol. III., p. 100. Mr. Bancroft further says, that Dudley "tried to destroy the liberties of Connecticut; prepared a volume of complaints; and urged the appointment of a Governor over Connecticut, by the royal prerogative," p. 70. It was about this time, or a little earlier, that a letter from his son, Paul Dudley, to the English court, was intercepted, in which he says: "This country, (New England), will never be worth living in for lawyers and gentlemen, *till the charter is taken away*. My father and I sometimes talk of the Queen's establishing a Court of Chancery in this country." See Hutchinson's History, Vol. II., p. 140.

tion in which he stood to the British crown," and in contradiction to the "principles which he had openly asserted and maintained." *

In the fourth place, Dr. Mather says: "I am afraid that the guilt of innocent blood is still crying in the ears of the Lord against you; I mean the blood of Leisler and Milburn." These men (Leisler and Milburn) were concerned in the revolution in New York, at the time of the accession of William and Mary, and were publicly executed, under sentence of Dudley, while he was Chief Justice of that province. Lord Bellamont afterwards declared, that "these men were not only murdered, but barbarously murdered." Mr. Bancroft also, in his history, speaks of their execution as "judicial murder."

Dr. Mather's fifth and last fear for the governor was, that "the Lord is offended with you, in that you ordinarily forsake the worship of God, in the holy church with which you are connected, in the afternoon of the Lord's day; and spend the whole time, after the public exercise, with some persons reputed very ungodly men."

In conclusion, Dr. Mather says: "How glad should I be, if I could receive satisfaction, that my fears of your being faulty in the matters I

* History Vol. I., p. 159.

have faithfully mentioned to you are groundless. But if it be otherwise, I am under pressure of conscience to bear a public testimony, without respect of persons; and shall rejoice if it may be my dying testimony. I am now aged, expecting and longing for my departure out of the world every day. I trust in Christ that, when I am gone, I shall obtain a good report of my having been faithful before him. To his mercy I commend you," &c.

Such is the letter of Increase Mather to Governor Dudley; a letter which, in the judgment of President Quincy, "breathes a spirit of *abuse* and *virulence*, of which the records of party animosity contain but few parallels." I have only to say, that I cannot so regard it; and I am sure that this community, when they come to understand the subject, will wonder that such language could have been used respecting it. For who, I must ask again, was this Governor Dudley? What was his character, in the estimation both of his cotemporaries, and of those who have come after him? Only a year before Dr. Mather's letter was written, a memorial was presented to "the Queen's most excellent Majesty," and signed by twenty of the more distinguished friends of New England, some in this country and some in London, accusing him of nothing less than *treason* ;—the supplying of the open enemies of his country with provisions and ammunition.

Governor Hutchinson says of Dudley: "Ambition was his ruling passion; and perhaps, like Cæsar, he had rather be the first man in New England, than the second in old. Mr. Alden Bradford represents him as one "covetous both of power and wealth, and as probably seeking for the former, as the best means of obtaining the latter." Mr. Bancroft says: "The character of Dudley was that of profound selfishness." He "loved neither freedom, nor his native land." He "is left without one to palliate his selfishness." President Quincy says that Dudley was "vindictive, craving, ambitious."

It was no disgrace to Dr. Mather, that he lost the favor of such a man; and that, before quite abandoning him, he was disposed to deal with him in a plain and faithful manner. With a fidelity like that of the old prophets in Israel, he tells the governor some painful truths, and points him forward to a coming judgment, which, in the midst of the cares and temptations of government, he was very liable to forget. On the whole, I think Dudley had more reason to be grateful for this letter, than to be angry at it;—more reason to thank the writer for his faithfulness, than to rail at him (as he did) for his rudeness and impertinence. And I think this letter of Dr. Mather one of the last things that should be seized upon, as furnishing ground of objection to his character.

It is further objected to Dr. Mather, that he was to a great and even ridiculous extent, the dupe of his own impressions,—impressions received, for the most part, in prayer, and which he deemed of an almost supernatural character. The impression of this kind which has been chiefly dwelt upon, and in the issue of which he was disappointed, was one which he cherished from about the year 1693, to the end of the century, with respect to an anticipated return to England. It was often impressed on him during this period, that "God would return him to England, and there give him opportunity, in some way, greatly to glorify the Lord Jesus Christ." He seems to have desired such an event, and in several instances the way was well nigh opened for the accomplishment of his wishes. But from various causes, he was disappointed. His accusers have seized hold of these impressions, and made them matter of ridicule and reproach. They talk of his "genuflexions, and prostrations, and spiritual elevations," and "glorious, heart-melting persuasions," in a manner which we deem offensive both to piety and taste; and finally resolve the whole into "the natural wishes of his own heart,—the cravings of an ambitious spirit."*

With regard to the subject here introduced, I remark, in the first place, that the current opinions and language of our fathers, in respect to various things, were so different from ours, that if we are disposed to take them out of their own age, and from among their cotemporaries, and judge of them by our standards, it is not difficult to make them appear ridiculous. For example, if all that the apostolic Eliot said and wrote respecting the abomination of wearing wigs and long hair, were collected together, how easy it would be to turn him into ridicule. Or if Governor Winthrop's account of the terrible judgment which befell Mrs. Dyer, in consequence of her having imbibed the errors of Mrs. Hutchinson, were copied out, and held prominently up to the gaze and disgust of modern eyes, not only the excellent governor, but many of his cotemporaries, might be made to appear ridiculous enough. But it may be questioned whether such a procedure would be fair or generous. And I have the same scruples as to the pro-

* Quincy's History, Vol. I., pp. 81—109.

priety of ransacking the diaries of the Mathers, in search of materials for ridicule and reproach, and especially for turning into ridicule their more secret and solemn acts of devotion.

But to come nearer to the subject in hand. While I dissent entirely from much that has been written, in our own times, in respect to what has been called "the prayer of faith," as being not only unscriptural, but of dangerous tendency, I still believe that there is such a thing as communion with God in prayer; yes, intimate, heart-melting, heart-dissolving communion,—such as the venerable Mather sometimes enjoyed, when he prostrated himself in secret before God, and wet his study floor with tears. I believe, too, that Christians who abound in prayer have sometimes such *sensible assistance* in their supplications for particular favors, that they can hardly resist the conclusion, when they rise from the duty, that the things prayed for will be bestowed. For they reason thus: "God would not have afforded me such *special* assistance in praying for this or that event, if he had not intended to hear the prayer, and grant the request." I see nothing enthusiastical, or unreasonable in a conclusion such as this; though, to be sure, we are not infallible in judgments of this nature, and they should be formed and followed with much prudence and caution.

I will go further and say, that if holy, spiritual persons, while engaged in their devotions, should think that they received remarkable impressions from God, with respect to certain coming events, I would not ridicule them. I would not say that the thing was impossible; for I know "there are more things in heaven and earth, than some men have dreamed of in their philosophy." I know, too, that some of the best Christians on earth have received such impressions, and that the things of which they were in this way premonished have often come to pass. Repeated instances of this kind, some of which have before been noticed, are alleged to have occurred in the life of Dr. Mather. At the same time I should feel, that even the best Christians were exceedingly liable to be deceived in regard to impressions of this nature; and consequently, that they should say but little about them, and more especially that they should not suffer their *duties*,—their conduct to be much influenced by them.

After this general expression of opinion, let us return to the case of the Mathers. I class them both together, because they were both alike concerned in this matter. In the first place, they were both of them *eminently persons of prayer*. They observed more private fasts, and vigils, and spent more time in their secret devotions,—I believe far more—than was common with Christians in their own age;—certainly more than is common now. And not only so, there was, if we may judge from their private writings, a *spirit*, a *fervor* in their devotions, a nearness and intimacy of communion with God, which has rarely been attained in this world of sin.

These men believed, not only in the duty, but in the *efficacy* of prayer. They *expected answers* to their prayers. Not unfrequently they had strong impressions, amounting almost to an assurance, that certain events in providence were about to take place. And in some instances they did take place. Men may account for such dispensations as they will; of the fact of their occurrence there can be no reasonable doubt. Still, Dr. Mather was liable to be deceived by his impressions; and in regard to his anticipated return to England, he certainly was deceived. Yet I see nothing in this, which should justly expose him to ridicule or reproach. This particular impression seems to have exerted little or no influence,—certainly no *bad* influence on his conduct. He might have returned to England in several instances, if he had been so disposed. The corporation of college repeatedly desired him to go to England on an agency for them; and in one instance, "the representatives and the governor voted a concurrence." At a later period, "the ministers of the province, by their delegates assembled at Boston, unanimously desired him to take a voyage to England, with an address from them," on the accession of George I., and "made provision for the expenses of the voyage."* But in neither of these cases, did the way in providence seem to him to be open. His duty was not plain. And until it was plain, his impression could have no influence to induce him to go. His recorded feelings in reference to the whole matter was: "Lord, if it will be more to *thy glory* that I should go to England, than for me to continue here in this land, then let me go; otherwise not." "The Lord overrule this affair to his own glory, and so that I may see his holy hand pointing me what I should do." Here, surely, is an unfeigned and entire submission to the will of God;—a feeling as unlike as possible to the restless longings of a selfish mind—"the cravings of an ambitious spirit."

* Remarkables, &c., p. 194.

I cannot conclude this topic in words more appropriate than those of Cotton Mather himself. "Christians, reproach not a *particular faith*, as if there never were a gracious work of heaven in it. But yet be cautioned against laying too much stress upon it, lest ye find yourselves incautiously plunged into a hope that will make ashamed. A particular faith *may be* a work of God; but the counterfeits of this jewel are so very fine, that it will require a judgment almost more than human to discern them. It is best that you should be content with the ordinary satisfaction of praying and waiting for the blessings of God, in such pious resignation to *his* will, and annihilations of *your own*, as an uncertainty about issues would most probably lead you to."*

Our modern accusers of Dr. Mather charge him with being influenced, almost perpetually, by *worldly*, *selfish*, and *ambitious motives*. And they think themselves fully entitled to do this, because, in consequence of having access to his diary, they know the motives by which he was influenced. "Of the motives and master-passions of his eventful presidency, we are enabled," says President Quincy, "to speak with

---

*Remarkables, &c., p. 195.

great certainty." "President Mather and his son both kept diaries, in which they have recorded their motives and purposes; so that in relation to either, there can hardly be any mistake."*

In reference to this sort of diary evidence, of which President Quincy has made so much use, I feel bound, in passing, to offer a few remarks. And I ask, in the first place, is it quite fair and honorable to bring out, in this way, the diaries of distinguished men? These diaries were written, not for the public eye, but for their own private inspection; or at most, for the inspection of some few personal, family friends. Is it right, then, to lay hold of them, and drag them out before the public, and turn them to a use for which they never were intended? Most men say things at their own firesides, and in presence of their families, which they would not wish to have published to the world. And if some impertinent listener were to treasure them up, and make them public, who would not be disposed to complain of the injury? We know not that President Quincy keeps a diary, but doubtless he is in the habit of writing letters, and maintaining a social, confidential corres-

*Quincy's History, Vol. I, p. 56.

pondence with his friends. And in the course of this correspondence, he may have written as few things unsuitable for the public eye, as any other individual. But would he be willing that, some hundred and fifty years hence, his private letters should be collected, and that the whole of them, or the more objectionable parts should be spread out to public view? Would he be willing that his successors in office should treat *him* after this manner, and to rest his permanent reputation on the result of such disclosures?

Almost all ministers, and many others, in the days of the Mathers were in the habit of keeping journals or diaries, in which they recorded their private thoughts, their religious impressions, and the more important transactions of their lives. But would it be right for their successors and descendants, into whose hands these private papers may have fallen, to make an indiscriminate exhibition of them before the world? As well might they strip their venerable ancestors of their wigs and doublets, and send them into the streets in shirts and night-caps.

Besides; the real import of the diaries of evangelical Christians is not unfrequently misunderstood, especially by those who do not sympathize with them in their religious feelings and views. Such Christians record, in their closets, the sense they feel of their many imperfections, and their great sinfulness in the sight of God; and persons who have less conscience of sin than they, and less sorrow for it, infer from the record, either that they were gross hypocrites, or that they had secretly been guilty of abominable crimes. Thus Boswell, finding in Johnson's diary, frequent intimations of his great sinfulness, and of the depth of his self-abasement, inferred that he must have been, secretly, a very wicked man. And Mr. Bancroft has no doubt, from Cotton Mather's account of his temptations and repentings, that his conscience troubled him for the part he had taken against the witches.

I once knew a man who bitterly hated what he termed "the Evangelicals," and because he had little else to allege against them, he used to appeal, for evidence, to their prayers. "Go and hear the wretches pray. We need no further evidence of guilt. They confess themselves to have committed the most abominable crimes." There was about as much sense and justice in this kind of reasoning, as in the conclusions that are sometimes drawn from the humble confessions of Christians in their diaries. Because Job "abhorred himself and repented in dust and ashes," and Isaiah confessed himself to be "a man of unclean lips," and Paul groaned habitually under a conscious burthen of sin, is it to be inferred that these holy men were hypocrites, and that they lived in the indulgence of palpable wickedness?

But I have not yet done with this species of diary evidence. When the diary does not treat of religious experience, but of the common affairs of life, there is reason to receive the testimony with much caution and allowance. For what is this testimony? It is not that of an individual under oath. Neither is it the word of one who is writing a history—writing for posterity,—stating what he has thoroughly examined, and knows to be fact. In the sensible language of the North American Review: "The writer of a diary puts down his present impressions, which may be materially erroneous, for want of the explanations which a little more time may bring. Where friendships or dislikes are concerned, or questions of conduct are at issue, he makes his record under the influence of feelings which may bias him from the juster conclusions of a cooler hour. At all events, if his testimony is to be produced, when both he, and they who may be harmed by it, are no more, it is simply the testimony of a witness who cannot be cross-examined, against one accused who cannot speak for himself;—a kind of evidence which no acknowledged principle or process of justice approves."* In proof of the justness of these remarks, it may be observed, that the diaries quoted by President Quincy not unfrequently contradict one another. Mather contradicts Sewall, and Sewall Leverett, and Leverett one, if not both the others. They all give their honest impressions at the time; but these impressions do not always coincide, and are to be received, as I said, with much caution and allowance.

I have offered these remarks, more because they seemed to be demanded by the general subject, than because of their necessity in order to a vindication of Dr. Mather. President Quincy "is enabled to speak with great certainty of his motives and master-passions," because he has got possession of his diary, or of certain parts of it; and under the shelter of such a caption, he proceeds to accuse his venerable predecessor of acting from selfish, base, ambitious motives, in many of the more important transactions of his life. Take the following instances as examples: Dr. Mather is said to have recanted his first thoughts respecting the half-way covenant, because "the side he had embraced

* For 1841, p. 353.

proved to be neither *popular* nor *prevailing.*" He changed his mind on the subject of toleration, *for the same reason.* It was " love of *distinction,*" in part, which led him to oppose the usurpations of Andros,—Vol. I, pp. 119—121. Again, when the new charter of government had gone into operation, and "the Calvinistic leaders of the province" which " Increase and Cotton Mather *aspired* to become "—" began to realize that the sceptre they had so long possessed had passed from their hands," they " sought to possess themselves of such *other instruments of power as were yet within their grasp ;*" and this was the secret of their strong attachment to the college,—pp. 65, 66. And when the college charter, which President Mather had exerted himself to push through the provincial legislature, and under which the corporation had acted long enough "to *gratify* him with a doctorate," was negatived by the king, President Quincy thinks it likely that Mather was *glad of it;* " as the affairs of the college were thrown into a state of inexplicable embarrassment," and " *the sense of the importance of his experience and services was greatly augmented,*"—p. 71. His opposition to the founders of the Brattle Street Church was the result of an " *excited temper,* and *wounded pride,*" and a desire to retain his *popularity* with the prevailing sect,"—p. 133. He was compelled, however, for prudential reasons, so far "to *smother* his resentments, as to take part in the religious services at the dedication of the church,"—p. 135.

Such is a specimen of the manner in which President Quincy goes on, through more than a hundred pages, imputing the basest motives to Dr. Mather, and representing him as a vile hypocrite, who cared nothing for college, church, or country; whose only concern was, so to conduct affairs that his own private ends might be answered, his own wrongs avenged, and the sense of his own personal importance and influence augmented. And his accuser feels fully authorized to make such representations, because he has had sight of Dr. Mather's diary, and is "able to speak with *certainty* as to the motives and master-passions of his eventful presidency."

But where is the evidence from the diary that such *were* "the master-passions" by which he was moved? Does Mather confess as much as this? Does he record it in his diary? As President Quincy has been pleased to appeal to the diary, we may insist that he should abide by it. He should, at least, so far abide by it, as in no instance directly to *contradict it*. And yet this he has very frequently done. In many instances, he imputes motives to Dr. Mather, the very *opposite* of those which the diary affirms. For example, Dr. Mather, in his diary, continually assigns it as his motive, and his only motive, for desiring to return to England, that he might there have an opportunity to glorify God, and serve the cause and the kingdom of Christ. But President Quincy can see nothing here but "the natural cravings of an *ambitious* spirit." Again, Dr. Mather, in his diary, repeatedly, and with the utmost apparent sincerity, expresses the determination to resign his office in college. He did this in 1695; and was prevented from carrying his determination into effect, only by the remonstrances of the corporation against it. He did the same, in three several instances, in 1697. Under date of August 7th, he says in his diary, "I am determined to resign my relation to the college the next week, having desired a corporation meeting for that end." "September 3d. My discouragements are such, that I am fully purposed to resign the presidentship." "September 15. At college to attend a corporation meeting, when I intended to resign the presidentship; but it being a stormy day, there wanted one to make a sufficient number for a meeting." Yet President Quincy persists in insinuating, if not asserting, that "these threats of resigning were intended only for effect, and that there was no sincerity in them,"—p. 96. Our charge here is, and it is an unanswerable charge, that having appealed to the diary as the grand source of evidence by which to decide upon the motives of his predecessor, President Quincy persists in imputing to him unworthy and selfish motives, not only without the evidence of the diary, but in *direct contradiction to it.* He will appeal to the diary, so long as any thing there recorded, by being distorted, perverted, and judged of by our modern standards, can be turned into matter of ridicule or invective; but when the diary assumes another character, it can be readily dispensed with, or directly contradicted.

I only remark further, in reference to President Quincy's treatment of Dr. Mather, that he represents him frequently, if not generally, as being actuated by a *wrong spirit,* as a *disturber* of the churches, as being rather a *bad* than a good man. Both to him and his son, "controversy was not so much an incident, as an *element* of their natures." Their theological zeal was always at the boiling point. Their controversy with the innovators of the times was conducted "neither with *temper* nor policy,"—pp. 132, 137.

"Violent doctrinal dissensions were by them excited and perpetuated" in the churches, through a long course of years,"*—p. 349. Of Increase Mather himself it is said, that in his controversy respecting church order, he "lost all *patience* and *self-possession*," and "was led to the exhibition of *great violence* and *personality*,"—pp. 133, 139. In a word, the character of Dr. Mather is summed up by President Quincy, in the following terms: He "was *restless*, *obtrusive*, *excitable*, *boastful* of his public services, and *complaining* of neglect and ingratitude." His whole life had been one "series of theological and political controversy." He "was a partisan by profession; always harnessed, and ready, and restless for the onset; now courting the statesman, now mingling with the multitude, exciting the clergy in the Synod, the congregation in the pulpit, and the people in the halls of the popular assembly,"—p. 147.

Of wholesale charges such as these, it would be useless to go into a particular examination. The most of them, it is well known, are false and slanderous; and the author of them, so long as they are permitted to stand unretracted, can

* What "*doctrinal* dissensions?" The Congregational ministers and churches of that period and for a long while afterwards, were agreed in doctrine.

in no way escape the imputation of being a libeller of the holy dead. Increase Mather's whole life "one series of theological and political *controversy!*" And yet of his eighty-six publications, more than seventy, as we shall presently see, are of a decidedly *practical character.* Increase Mather a *disturber* of the New England churches and clergy! And yet Dr. Eliot describes him as "the *father* of the New England clergy, whose name and character were held in *veneration*, not only by those who knew him, but by succeeding generations." It was this same slandered Increase Mather, who (to use the language of the General Court,) by "unwearied, indefatigable labor and service, voluntarily undertaken for the good of his country, and attended with much difficulty and hazard to his person," saved Massachusetts from revolution and bloodshed, and gave to her a charter of government, under which she prospered for almost a century. This, too, is the man, (and with some, this is his great and unpardonable offence,) who, by his resistance to unscriptural and alarming innovations, kept back the tide of spiritual desolation from rolling over the churches of the Pilgrims for a series of years, and greatly restricted its ravages, when at length it came;—the man, to whom New England is more indebted, ecclesiastically and civilly, than to any other individual who ever lived in it; who, when he died, was "honored with a greater funeral than had ever been seen in these parts of the world," and in consequence of whose death, "the pulpits, throughout the country, rang with mingled eulogies and funeral lamentations."*

One of the most painful effects of President Quincy's misrepresentations is the impression which they left on the mind of the late learned and estimable Mr. Grahame, author of a History of the United States. Though not a Puritan by descent, Mr. Grahame was evidently one in feeling. He was a Calvinist of the Scottish church, and seems to have been a truly pious man. He had a strong sympathy with the early settlers of New England, and in his History had spoken in the most favorable terms of the Mathers. He calls Increase Mather "the most eminent theologian, and the most pious and popular minister of Massachusetts." But after reading Quincy's History of Harvard University, he hardly knew what to say or to think. We find the following passage in his Journal: "He (President Quincy) wounds my prejudices by attacking the Mathers, and other persons of

*Remarkables &c., p. 211.

a primitive cast of Puritanism, with a severity the more painful to me, that I see not well how I can demur to its justice." And in a note, in the last edition of his History, Mr. Grahame says: "From President Quincy's History of Harvard University, it appears to me, much more clearly than agreeably, that, in the instance of Cotton Mather, as well as of his father, a strong and acute understanding, though united with real piety, was sometimes corrupted by a deep vein of passionate vanity and absurdity."* Had Mr. Grahame lived long enough to learn the real character of President Quincy's History, and the little credit which is due to it, more especially on points which conflict with the author's religious prejudices, his good opinion of the Mathers would not have been much affected by such an authority.

But we leave the venerated Increase Mather to his rest. It will not be disturbed, nor will his reputation permanently suffer, by any attempts, at this late day, to tarnish and reproach it. The shafts of his revilers will recoil and fasten on themselves, rather than fall with lasting injury on him.

---

* Memoir, p. 24. Hist. vol. I, p. 289.

CHAPTER XI.

Abstract of Cotton Mather's Sermon, on the death of his father. Catalogue of Increase Mather's publications.

I HAVE before stated, that the sermon at the funeral of Dr. Mather was preached by the Rev. Mr. Foxcroft, of the first church. But this was not the only funeral sermon. The ministers of Boston all delivered discourses on occasion of his death; and not only in Boston, but "throughout the country, the pulpits rang with mingled eulogies and funeral lamentations."

The fact that so many sermons were preached on the occasion, is proof of the *deep veneration* in which the deceased patriarch was held; and the sermons themselves, could we have access to them, would furnish the best means of forming a due estimate of his character. But these discourses, like their authors, have passed away. They are treasured up in the book of God's account, but (so far as I know, with a single exception) they are no longer accessible to the living. The exception to which I refer is the sermon of

Cotton Mather, preached to the Old North Church, in Boston, September 8th, 1723, the second Sabbath after his father's death. The greater part of this discourse is preserved; and I know not how I can more appropriately conclude the Memoir of Increase Mather, than by presenting my readers with an abstract of it. It will be interesting, not only on account of the preacher and the solemn circumstances under which it was preached, but as exhibiting the topics on which Increase Mather had chiefly insisted, during his long ministry.

The preacher commences in his peculiar, quaint, characteristic manner, as follows: "My design this day is, to preach over some *thousands* of sermons; and yet I design but *one short sermon* for you. My design is, to preach over the sermons of *another man;* and yet the sermon shall be honestly and entirely *my own.* My design is, to give pungency to a ministry of which God has now deprived us; and to apply over again the goads which the late master of our assemblies had used upon us; or to clench the golden nails which, for more than three score years together, he has been driving into us. I shall endeavor that the word of the gospel, as he preached it to you, may endure forever in your affectionate remembrance; yea, more than this, that it may be retained in the hands of your children after you.

"The advice given to the church at Sardis, Rev. 3: 3, may be a very proper introduction to my undertaking: '*Remember how thou hast received and heard.*'"

DOCTRINE.

A people ought to remember what they have heard preached unto them, and how they have received it.

After opening and discussing the doctrine of the text, the preacher proceeded to make application of it, as follows:

"In the ministry of your departed pastor, there were some articles of a more frequent and cogent inculcation, whereof you will allow me to be, this day, a remembrancer unto you. Though he preached over the whole body of divinity, and occasional subjects without number, yet there were all along *some* articles which in the fulfilling of his ministry, he pressed with a peculiar flame; and I hope you will apprehend *him* speaking to you, in my brief recapitulation of them.

"1. Remember how you have received and heard, that *sin is an odious and a dangerous evil.* Your late pastor began his ministry here with several sermons on Lam. 5: 16. '*Wo is unto us, that we have sinned;*' wherein he discoursed on the *woful effects of sin.* And although few now alive remember those sermons, yet this you may all remember, that the unknown and too much unregarded and unlamented *evil of sin* was what his ministry did exceedingly mind you of. What pains did he take to convince you, that none but fools make a mock at sin; that it is a most vile thing, by sin, to deny the God above; and that no sinner can hope to go unpunished. How vehemently did he, as with the hammer which breaketh the rock in pieces, drive this home upon you, that *no sin is to be indulged or harbored,* nor so much as a sinful thought to be allowed a lodgment within you. How often has he declared it unto you, that *one known sin, lived in, is incompatible with a state of salvation;* that it will be leak enough to sink the soul that persists in it. What mighty thunderings have you heard from this pulpit, as from a flaming mountain, against those things, for which the wrath of God comes on the children of disobedience? What warnings was he accustomed to give against those particular sins, by which he saw that the souls of men were most endangered? O remember these things, and from the words of his lips learn to keep yourselves from the paths of the destroyer.

"2. Remember how you have received and heard, that *a real and sound conversion to God is the one thing of all others most needful for you.* The sermons which your late pastor preached, and which have been several times printed, on Mat. 18: 3. 'Except ye be converted, and become as little children, ye shall not enter into the kingdom of heaven;' these were not the only sermons in which he pressed upon you the necessity of turning and of living unto God. That alienation from God which the fall has brought upon us was so grievous unto him, that the necessity of regeneration seemed a thing that could not be too frequently or too earnestly pleaded for. With what loud calls and peals did he thunder it in your ears, that you *must* have a work of grace wrought in you, and a holiness, without which no man shall see the Lord; that you must have experience of the *new birth,* or good had it been for you if you had never been born; that you *must* become new creatures, else he that made you will not have mercy on you, and he that formed you will show you no favor. And then, like the angel that hastened the lingerers out of Sodom, how zealously, terribly did he call on the delaying sinner, '*Fly for thy life!*' The word with him was, '*To-day! to-day! to-day!*' Can you forget the piercing sound of it? The uncertain approaches and surprises of certain death, and the madness of resisting the Holy Spirit on whose influences your conversion depends; how powerfully, earnestly were you minded of these things!

"Then, as he had been himself a pattern of early piety, and in the close of his days, there was no one thing that so much comforted him as this, '*I gave* myself up to God in my youth;' so he was a most fervent and winning preacher to the young. Early piety! how mightily, how ardently, and with what frequent excitations, did he plead for this! O children and youth, remember these things; and know that you are deaf to thunder, if you can still continue in your unregeneracy.

"3. Remember how you have received and heard, that *persons may go very far, and seem very fair, in a profession of religion, and after all be hypocrites and castaways.* It was with a singular agony that your late pastor, many years ago, preached several sermons on Job 27: 8. 'What is the hope of the hypocrite?' And how often since, and in how many sermons, and with what an unparalleled solemnity, has he told you, that many *seem* to be religious, whose religion is vain? That many flatter themselves with vain expectations to be found among the blessed of the Lord, who, after all, shall be led forth with the workers of iniquity! That many pass through awakenings, convictions, and contritions, and come even to reformations, and some consolations, who yet, for want of closing with Christ in all his offices, and for the sake of some lust from which they are not willing to be divorced, find themselves miserably deceived at the last. How pathetically would he bewail the fate of these poor self-deceivers! O remember these things, and let us beware that we be not found among the sinners in Zion!

"4. Remember how you have received and heard, that *to pray always is the best and surest means of good.* Your late pastor not only preached (what you have on your shelves) his discourses on Psalm 32: 6. 'Every one that is godly *will pray;*' but you have heard it from him in his preaching a thousand times, that prayer is the *first note* of a soul returning to God; that, without prayer, there is nothing to be done, and no good to be looked for; that prayer is the *main engine* with which all good purposes are to be carried on. Prayer was that which he himself used with an unceasing assiduity; and he preached it, as he used it. He had witnessed amazing answers to prayers. The efficacy of prayer was demonstrated and exemplified to admiration in what he had himself experienced; and this added flame to the heat with which he would have melted you to run into the like devotions. How potently have you heard *secret* prayer commended to you, as that to which it is impossible that any child of God should be a stranger? How forcibly, and with what an arrest upon the conscience, have you heard *household* prayer demanded of you? And with what thunderings and lightnings have you heard that voice of God ringing in your ears: 'Pour out thy fury upon the families that call not on thy name.' O remember these things; and let none of you be those inexcusable workers of iniquity, who call not upon God!

"5. Remember how you have received and heard, that *the table of the Lord is to be seriously and thoughtfully prepared for, and worthily approached.* It was a grief to your late pastor, to see so many turn their backs upon the table of the Lord; thus openly proclaiming that, after all the means which have been used for them, the case of their souls is yet in a wretched uncertainty. He pressed the plain command of the Saviour, '*Do this* in remembrance of me;' and could not see why any should be so afraid of disobeying the command by coming unsuitably, as to shake off all fear of disobedience by not coming at all. At the same time, he strongly urged the necessity of *preparation*. He did not look on the supper of the Lord as a *converting* ordinance. The bread, he said, belonged to none but *the children*. How powerfully did he preach on Matt. 22: 12. 'How camest thou in hither, not having on a wedding garment?' A process of *repentance* was the first thing to be gone through with; and then he proposed an *additional* preparation, incumbent on those who are already the children of God. Accordingly, it was his own custom, for three-score years together, to spend a whole day in secret prayer and fasting, before the celebration of the holy supper. O remember these things; and let none of you dare come to the table of the Lord unworthily, and thus eat and drink judgment to yourselves.'

"6. Remember how you have received and heard, when *the eternity*, to which we are all hastening, has been held up before you. Of what did your late pastor more frequently remind you, than *eternity?* That word *eternity*, he often said, is enough to break the heart of any one, that will solemnly think of it. With what anticipations of the last trump, and the final doom, did you hear him preach on Heb. 9 : 27. 'And after death *the judgment.*' You have seen him opening the bars of the pit, and setting before you, in the most awful colors, the second death; bringing up the damned from their place of torment, and showing you the ever burning lake. You have seen him removing as it were the screen, and giving you a sight of the fire that never shall be quenched; that so, knowing the terrors of the Lord, you may be persuaded into the way of understanding, and not go down to the congregation of the dead.

"You have also seen heaven opened, in the discoveries which he thence brought to you, concerning the worship of God above by myriads of angels, and the spirits of the just made perfect, with Jesus the Mediator of the new covenant, carried on in the true temple above;—discoveries of the rest from the days of evil, and the fullness of joy and pleasures forevermore, to be enjoyed in the blissful mansions. He drew aside the vail, and showed you the interior of the holy place, that so he might persuade you to accompany him in the way to Zion, with your faces thitherward. O remember these things, and flee from the wrath to come! Remember, and lay hold on eternal life!

"7. Remember, especially, how you have received and heard, concerning *a glorious Christ, the enthroned, the incarnate, the infinite Son of God.* Your late pastor knew very well how to preach—and he did it more than once—on Col. 3: 11. '*Christ is all, and in all.*' In his entire ministry, he *made* him so, determining to know nothing but Christ and him crucified. You never saw him so much in his element, as when the glories of Christ were to be set before you. The doctrine of Christ was the grand theme, to which he advised those who were to become preachers of the gospel; and he set an example in this respect well worthy to be imitated. Remember what you have so often heard about the importance of *accepting* a glorious Christ, with all his benefits, as offered in the gospel; and about the way of *living* on a glorious Christ, in all that you have to *do* and *suffer*, while you are living in this dying world; and about the manner of living *to* Christ, as well as on him, if you would be able to say, 'For me to die shall be gain.' O let the remembrance of these things make you well established Christians."

"But I have now done. What I have this day preached to you must be called a sermon *to bring to remembrance.* Like Peter the aged, I have hoped to stir up your pure minds, by way of *remembrance.* It was charged upon the Hebrews as a fault: 'Ye have *forgotten* the exhortation which speaketh unto you, as unto children.' O my dear people, on whom the doctrine of your late pastor dropped as the rain, and distilled as the dew, as the small rain upon the tender herb, and as the showers upon the grass; see to it that this fault shall never be charged home upon you!"

I have presented this long extract, both as an index of the preaching of Increase Mather, and a specimen of the style and manner of his son. A few of the expressions have been modernized, but the plan, the thoughts, and in general the language, are all his own. And in view of it I cannot repress the inquiry, When, where, was any church more soundly instructed, more richly fed, than was the Old North Church in Boston, under the ministry of the Mathers? We talk of improvements in the manner of preaching; and in some respects there have been improvements. But it becomes us to inquire, whether in other respects, we have not deteriorated, and whether the effects of the deterioration are not visible around us. When the great, stirring truths and facts of the gospel are pressed home upon the minds, and the hearts of a people, with the point, the spirit, the unction of the Mathers, they always have been followed—they always *will be*—with glorious results.

It only remains that I present, as a memorial of the industry and piety of Dr. Mather, a simple, chronological catalogue of his published works. Not a few of the publications, whose titles follow, passed through several editions.

1669.

The Mystery of Israel's Salvation.

1670.

The Life and Death of the Rev. Richard Mather.

1673.

Woe to the Drunkards.

1674.

The Day of Trouble near.

Important Truths about Conversion.

1675.

The First Principles of New England.

A Discourse concerning Baptism, and the Consociation of Churches.

The Wicked Man's Portion.

The Times of Men in the Hands of God.

1676.

A History o the War with the Indians; with an Exhortation to the Inhabitants.

1677.

A Relation of the Troubles of New England from the Indians, from the Beginning.

An Historical Discourse on the Efficacy of Prayer.

Renewal of Covenant, the Duty of Decaying and Distressed Churches.

1678.

Pray for the Rising Generation.

1679.

A Call to the Rising Generation.

1680.

The Divine Right of Infant Baptism.

The Great Concernment of a Covenanting People.

Heaven's Alarm to the World.

1682.

A Diatribe concerning the Sign of the Son of Man (in Latin).

Practical Truths, in Several Sermons.

The Church, a Subject of Persecution.

1683.

Cometographia; or a Discourse concerning Comets.

1684.

Remarkable Providences.

The Doctrine of Divine Providence.

1685.

An Arrow against Profane and Promiscuous Dances.

1686.

The Mystery of Christ.

The greatest of Sinners Exhorted.

A Sermon on the Execution of a poor man for Murder.

1687.

A Testimony against Superstitions.

1688.

A Letter concerning the Success of the Gospel among the Indians, (in Latin).*

1689.

The Unlawfulness of using Common Prayer, and of Swearing on the Book.

1690.

Several Papers relating to New England.

A Relation of the State of New England.

The Revolution Justified.

1693.

The Blessing of Primitive Counselors, (an Election Sermon).

Cases of Conscience concerning Witchcraft.

An Essay on the Power of the Pastor for the Administration of the Sacraments.

---

* Addressed to Dr. John Leusden of Utrecht.

1695.

Whether a Man may marry his Wife's Sister.

Solemn Advice to Young Men.

1696.

Angelographia; A Treatise of Angels.

1697.

A Discourse on Man's not knowing his Time.

The Case of Conscience concerning the Eating of Blood.

1698.

David Serving his Generation: A Funeral Sermon, for the Rev. John Bailey.

1699.

The Surest Way to the Highest Honor.

A Discourse on Hardness of Heart.

The Folly of Sinning.

1700.

The Order of the Gospel Vindicated.

1701.

The Blessed Hope.

1702.

Remarks on a Sermon of George Keith.

Ichabod: Or, the Glory Departing.

The Excellency of a Public Spirit.

The Righteous Man, a Blessing. Two Sermons.

1703.

The Duty of Parents to Pray for their Children.

Soul-saving Gospel Truths.

1704.

The Voice of God in Stormy Winds.

Practical Truths, to Promote Holiness.

1705.

Meditations on the Glory of Christ.

1706.

A Discourse concerning Earthquakes.

A Testimony against Sacrilege.

A Dissertation concerning the Right to the Sacrament.

1707.

Meditations on Death.

A Disquisition concerning the State of Souls Departed.

1709.

A Dissertation concerning the Future Conversion of the Jews. Confuting Dr. Lightfoot, and Mr. Baxter.

1710.

A Discourse concerning Faith, and Prayer for the Kingdom of Christ.

A Sermon on " Be very Courageous;" at the Artillery Election.

Awakening Truths, tending to Conversion.

1711.

Meditations on the Glory of the Heavenly World.

A Discourse concerning the Death of the Righteous.

The Duty of the Children of Godly Parents.

1712.

Burnings Bewailed.

Remarks upon an Answer to a Book against the Common Prayer.

Meditations on Sanctification of the Lord's Day.

1713.

A Plain Discourse, showing who shall, and who shall not, enter into Heaven.

The Believer's Gain by Death: A Funeral Sermon for his Daughter-in-Law.

1714.

Resignation to the Will of God. On the Death of his Consort.

1715.

Jesus Christ, a Mighty Saviour.

1716.

A Disquisition concerning Ecclesiastical Councils.

There is a God in Heaven.

The Duty and Dignity of Aged Servants of God.

1718.

The Duty of Praying for Ministers. A Sermon at the Ordination of his Grandson.

Sermons on the Beatitudes.

Practical Truths plainly delivered; an Ordination Sermon.

1719.

Five Sermons on Several Subjects. One on the Author's Birthday.

1721.

Advice to the Children of Godly Ancestors.

Tracts, on Inoculation for the Small Pox.

1722.

A Dying Pastor's Legacy.

Elijah's Mantle.

Besides these *eighty-six* publications, Dr. Mather wrote many fugitive pieces, and "learned and useful Prefaces," which the publishers of books obtained from him, sufficient, if col lected, to make a considerable volume.

LIFE OF SIR WILLIAM PHIPPS.

LIFE OF SIR WILLIAM PHIPPS.

CHAPTER I.

His parentage, and circumstances in early life. Becomes a ship-carpenter, and removes to Boston. His marriage. Exepdition to Sheepscot. His voyages of discovery in pursuit of wealth. His final success.

Some of the more striking peculiarities of New England character — traits which have come down to us from our Puritan ancestry—are *energy*, *enterprise*, *activity*, *perseverance*, in whatever we think proper to undertake. We are proverbially a scheming, stirring people, who, if we do not find business, can make it, and who, if we cannot live one way, can somehow contrive to live another. It is next to impossible to starve a genuine Yankee, or by any adverse change of circumstances effectually to put him down.

And yet, there are two sorts of characters,

even among ourselves; or rather, our people exhibit the above traits of character in very different degrees. Some, though of Puritan stock, and born and bred in New England, are well nigh destitute of the peculiarities referred to. They may be social, intelligent, virtuous, amiable, but they are not enterprising and persevering. They may not be palpably indolent or inefficient, but they are incapable of giving the right direction to things, and of carving out a portion for themselves.

At the other extreme from the persons here described, we find a very different exhibition of New England character. Here are men, whose inventive resources are well nigh exhaustless, and whose energy and perseverance are indomitable. It matters little to them in what condition of life they are placed. If circumstances favor, they make the most of them; or if otherwise, they rise above them. If an individual of this class is given to books, he can study as effectively at the blacksmith's forge, or by the kitchen candle, as others can in the best furnished apartments. Shut such an one up in prison, with nought but a jack-knife and a shingle, and he will soon have wrought out something which he hopes will sell. Or put him down on a naked rock in the ocean, and he will at once begin to collect earth upon it, prepare his garden, and make ready for some kind of commerce with the world.

It is to an individual of this latter class that I propose to direct attention in the following pages. Sir William Phipps was (in the comman, popular sense of the terms,) *the maker of his own fortune.* Commencing life under the most forbidding circumstances, he rose, by his own efforts, to the possession, not only of a great estate, but of the highest honors to which, in this country, he could at that time aspire;—and all this, without compromising his moral or Christian character, and without incurring more than a moderate share of the envy or hostility of the world. And yet he died at the early age of forty-four. The study of such a life and example cannot but be useful, more especially to my youthful readers. It will not be without interest, I hope, to all.

William Phipps, was born at Nequasset, (now Woolwich, Me.,) Feb. 2, 1651, almost two hundred years ago. His father, James Phipps, was, by occupation, a gunsmith. He emigrated from Bristol, England, at an early period in the settlement of this country, and fixed his residence at the place above mentioned, on the eastern bank of the Kennebec river, some twelve or fifteen miles from its mouth.

There had been for some years, an establishment at this place for fishermen and other adventurers; still, the settlement was new, and the inhabitants (what there were of them) were rude and uncultivated. They were surrounded on nearly all sides, by dense forests, of which wild beasts and wandering Tarratines were the joint proprietors; and which—with the exception of here and there a straggling Frenchman, or a Jesuit priest—had never been penetrated by civilized man.

Such was the place selected by James Phipps as his future home; and here he became the father, and that too by one wife, of no less than *twenty-six children*, twenty-one of whom were sons!! Of these, William was one of the youngest; and as his father died when he was a child, he was left almost entirely to the management of his mother. Of the religious character of this remarkable mother, of her domestic habits and qualities, of the manner in which she trained and disposed of her children, of her subsequent history, and of the time and manner of her death, we have almost no information. And as little do we know respecting the other members of this numerous household. It is stated that William was employed, chiefly, till his eighteenth year, in feeding and tending his mother's flocks. His business was to guard the pasture and the fold, and defend his charge from the inroads of wolves, and bears, and Indians. Meanwhile, it does not appear that he had ever been to school at all, or had learned so much as to read or write.

And here let us pause a moment, to contemplate the condition of this young man, and to compare it with that of the youth among ourselves. Hardly any circumstances can be conceived more discouraging and repellent than his. He was but one of twenty-six children, of poor parents, and his mother a widow. Of course, he had nothing to expect, by way of parental assistance or patrimony. It devolved on him to assist his widowed mother, rather than on her to do much for him. Then he was entirely without education, patronage, or powerful friends, and had enjoyed but few opportunities of becoming acquainted with the world. In these circumstances, who could have expected anything better of young Phipps, than that he should grow up in ignorance, become a squatter and a hunter, live and die a boor, and be forgotten?

But he early manifested that he had a *soul*

which could not be confined to Nequasset. He was ignorant of many things, indeed of most things; but he knew that he lived on the banks of a noble river, which rolled its waters into the great sea; and on that sea he longed to embark, and to pursue his fortune in other lands. This desire, however, did not prompt him, as it sometimes does inconsiderate youth, to abscond from the parental roof, and rush upon his course of adventure in disgrace. He would ship openly and honorably, or not at all; and as no opportunity of doing this immediately presented, he concluded, as his next best resource, to apprentice himself to a ship-carpenter.

For the next four years of his life we are to contemplate him, therefore, as a laboring mechanic;—in an honorable and useful employment, indeed, but one hardly comporting with his romantic and adventurous disposition. In one respect, however, he was an example to all succeeding apprentices. He did not rudely break his bonds, and desert his master, but served his time out to the end.

Up to this period, he had scarcely traveled, (so far as we know,) beyond the precincts of his native village; and his friends would fain have persuaded him to repress his roving spirit, and quietly settle among themselves. But to this he could not consent. He seems to have had a presentiment that he was made for something better than could ever be realized in Nequasset.

Accordingly, the next we hear of him is at Boston, where he worked at his trade about a year, employing his leisure hours in learning to read and write, and in acquiring the rudiments of arithmetic and navigation. In the course of this year, he received his first permanent *religious* impressions, under the preaching of Dr. Increase Mather. Before the end of the year, he became a husband.

His wife was the widow of a merchant by the name of Hull, and the daughter of Capt. Roger Spencer, of Saco. She was older than himself, and had some fortune; but for aught that appears, the connection was founded on mutual affection, and proved a permanently happy one. His course of life called him often away from the endearments of home, but he seems to have been, uniformly, a faithful and devoted husband.

The addition to his pecuniary means acquired by his marriage, enabled him to enter into business for himself. He contracted with several Boston merchants to build them a vessel on the Sheepscot river, and bring back with him a load of lumber. This is the first mention of the Maine lumber trade, which I have been able to discover in our early history. Phipps proceeded to the place of his destination, built his vessel, launched it, and was just ready to take in his cargo, when an opportunity presented to test the kindness and generosity of his disposition, though much to his pecuniary disadvantage. Instigated by the French, the Indians of those parts suddenly took up arms, and commenced plundering and destroying the white inhabitants; and to these defenceless inhabitants —some of them his former neighbors and family connections—young Phipps was now as a ministering angel. He abandoned his lumber, received them on board his vessel protected, and succored them free of charge, and carried them all safe to Boston. An act like this, in a man of small resources, just entering into life, is worthy to be recorded. It served to develope his spirit and character, and was no doubtful presage of his future greatness.

Of the next eight or ten years of Capt. Phipps' life, almost no incidents are recorded. His home was at Boston, but in what manner he spent his time, his biographer has not informed us. Of this we may be sure, however, that he was not idle; for he could not be. His mind was fruitful in schemes and enterprises, and he was diligently occupied one way or another.

Under the faithful preaching of the Mathers, he was, doubtless, acquiring religious knowledge; while at the same time he was improving his education, and growing in a knowledge of the world.

The period in our country's history of which we now speak was marked with some striking peculiarities. Men's minds were occupied with golden dreams, and not a few were rushing upon untried and absurd methods of procuring wealth. The success of the Spaniards in their mining operations led many to believe that the soil of New England covered vast quantities of gold and silver; and mining rods and other strange expedients were resorted to, to discover, if possible, the hidden treasure.

Piracies, too, were of continual occurrence; and if not countenanced, they were connived at, by some in authority. These were the days of such men as Joseph Bradish, and Robert Kidd, both of whom were apprehended in this country, and executed in England. Many believed that the pirates had secreted vast sums upon our shores, and instead of digging for money by the cultivation of their fields, they had recourse to dreamers and diviners to disclose to them the mysterious deposits. The absurd practice of money-digging commenced about these times;

a practice which even now has not entirely ceased.

It does not appear that Capt. Phipps ever sought to obtain wealth by any such methods. He had other and more feasible plans in view. He knew that, for a long course of years, Spanish vessels had been crossing the ocean, heavily laden with gold and silver. He knew the usual track of these vessels. He knew that several of them had been lost. And it occurred to him that it would be possible to discover some of these wrecks, and bring back from the deep a portion of that wealth which it had swallowed up. This certainly was a lawful, if not a laudable enterprise; and however it may strike the mind of an adventurer now, it appeared sufficiently promising, in that age, to engage the attention even of the government.

Phipps' first voyage of discovery was made in a small vessel of his own. He succeeded in finding the wreck he was in search of, but the amount of treasure recovered from it was scarcely sufficient to defray the expense of the undertaking.

Nothing discouraged, however, he prepared to renew the attempt, and to do it on a much larger scale. He proceeded to England, and laid his plans directly before the king, James II.

The plain, blunt manner of the New England sailor seems to have commended him to the royal favor; for he was immediately appointed to the command of the Rose Algier, a ship of eighteen guns and ninety-five men, with instructions to cruise among the West India Islands.

This expedition proved one of extreme hazard and difficulty to Capt. Phipps, owing to the mutinous and piratical character of his men. They are represented as "a motley and lawless crew, unused to the restraints of a ship of war," and intent only on the acquisition of gold; and whether this were obtained by might or right, it mattered little to them. They soon became wearied with groping after wealth on the bottom of the ocean, preferring rather to capture it on the surface. They insisted on commencing a piratical expedition against the Spanish vessels and towns. On one occasion, they broke out into open mutiny, drew their swords, and insisted that their commander should join them in their piracy, or lose his life; but he, to use the language of Mather, "though he had not so much of a weapon as an ox-goad or a jaw-bone, yet like another Shamgar or Sampson, rushed in among them, and with the blows of his bare hands felled a part of them, and quelled the rest." This account will not seem improbable, when it is recollected that Phipps was a man of gigantic stature and strength, as well as of the most undaunted bravery, before whose naked fists, when he became excited, a whole ship's crew of smaller and guilty men might be ready to quail.

On another occasion, Capt. Phipps had anchored his vessel near a small, uninhabited island, that it might undergo some repairs; and had removed his stores and a part of his guns to the shore. Under pretence of relaxation, the greater part of the crew had retired to the woods. While there, they formed a ring, and entered into a most solemn agreement that they would that very night seize the captain and his few friends, put them on shore and abandon them, take the vessel and the stores and go to seek their fortunes in the South seas. But the providence of God interposed to defeat them. They had sent for the ship's carpenter, acquainted him with their purpose, and solicited him to join the conspiracy. He asked for half an hour to consider the matter, and in the meantime went to the vessel, as if to fetch away his tools. Two or three of the conspirators accompanied him, to watch his motions. Soon after he came on board he feigned himself sick, and ran into the cabin, as if to get some medicine. He here found the captain alone, and in few words told him of the whole design. It was now towards evening, and Phipps had not more than two hours in which to prepare to meet his enemies; but his plan of operation was instantly formed. He directed the carpenter to go back to the crew, and in appearance to join them. He then rallied his few faithful friends, went on shore to the tent where he had deposited a part of his guns and his stores, drew the charges from the guns, wheeled them round, and brought away all the ammunition to the ship. He next loaded the guns which remained on board, and so leveled them that not one of the men on shore could get to the ship, or to the stores, without being instantly killed.

The mutineers soon made their appearance from the woods, but when they came near to the tent of provisions, and saw what had been done there, they cried out at once, *We are betrayed.* And they were confirmed in this, when they heard the captain calling out to them in a voice of thunder, to stand off, and saw him preparing to cut them down with his artillery. Perceiving that he now had them entirely in his power, and that he was intending to abandon them, as they had thought to abandon him, the wretches soon came to terms. They fell upon their knees, protesting that they had nothing against him, except his unwillingness to join them in their wicked designs. They humbly entreated forgiveness for the past, gave assurances of good behavior in future, and begged that they might be taken on board the ship. When he had sufficiently tried them, and secured their arms, he consented to receive them back; but being now satisfied that they were not to be trusted, he soon sailed for Jamaica, and turned them off. In their place he embarked a few men, just to manage the ship, and almost immediately returned to England.

Notwithstanding his want of success in the immediate object of his expedition, Phipps was received with favor both by the admiralty and the king. He had proved himself to be a brave and a trustworthy commander. He had accomplished all that, under the circumstances, could have been reasonably expected. He had defeated the mutinous designs of his crew, and, at the imminent hazard of life, had saved a national vessel from becoming a marauder and a pirate.

Before leaving the West Indies, Capt. Phipps had heard, from an old Spaniard, the story of a wreck which occurred some fifty years before; and had satisfied himself as to *the place* of its occurrence. It was on a reef of rocks a few leagues to the north of Port de la Plata, which is one of the ports of Hispaniola. He had even visited the spot himself, but without the time or the means for a thorough investigation. He was extremely anxious, therefore, to return, and to make one more attempt to recover the lost treasures of the deep. He hoped, for this purpose, to be put again in command of a national ship; but in this he was disappointed. The government was unable or unwilling to undertake any more adventures of this nature. He next endeavored to interest some private individuals in the enterprise; and in this he was more successful. The Duke of Albemarle, in connection with a few others, consented at last to fit out a vessel, and to give him the command of it. A tender was furnished, to make short excursions in places where the ship could not go. Various necessary implements were also provided, some of which were not only contrived, but constructed by Phipps himself. The king's patent was obtained, giving to the associates an exclusive right to all the wrecks that might be discovered, reserving but a tithe as the royal portion.

All things being in readiness, he set sail from London for Port de la Plata, where he speedily and safely arrived. Before commencing operations, he constructed, from the trunk of a huge cotton tree, a long boat, capable of carrying some fifteen or twenty men. In this labor, as in every other, he bore a part, swinging the adze and the axe with his own hand. "A number of the men, with some Indian divers, were now despatched in the tender to the reef, while the captain and the rest of the crew remained with the ship. Having anchored the tender at a convenient distance, the men proceeded in the boat to examine the rocks, which they were well able to do on account of the clearness and calmness of the sea."

"The reef was of a singular form, rising nearly to the surface; but the sides fell off so precipitously that a ship striking them must necessarily have bounded back, and sunk in deep water. Hoping to find the wreck lodged on some projecting shelf of the rock, the men rowed round it several times, and sent down the divers in different places. At the same time they hung over the sides of the boat, and strained their eyes in gazing downwards, to discover, if possible, some fragment of the ship. All, however, was in vain, and they were preparing to return to the tender. But just as they were about to leave the place, one of the men perceiving a curious sea plant, called a feather, growing in the crevice of the rocks, sent down one of the

Indians to pluck it. When the diver returned, he told them that he saw a number of great guns lying in the same spot. Other divers were immediately sent down, and soon one brought up a large ingot of silver, worth from two to three hundred pounds sterling. Overjoyed at their success, they marked the spot with a buoy, and then returned with the boat and tender to the ship."

That they might the more agreeably surprise the captain, the men first told him a discouraging story, pretending that they had met with no success. But while they were talking, he chanced to spy the ingot of silver which they had placed under the table; upon which he exclaimed, in an agony of earnestness, "Why, what is this? Whence comes this?" And then they told him all the truth. After hearing their story, Phipps lifted up his hands and said, "Thanks be to God! Now we are all made!"

"The whole crew were immediately set to work, and in the course of a few days they fished up treasures from the ocean to the amount of three hundred thousand pounds sterling; not less than a million and a half of dollars! They first lighted on that part of the wreck where the bullion was stored, and which was brought up in *solid ingots*—called by the sailors *sows and pigs.* But they afterwards fell upon the coin, which had been stored in bags among the ballast. "It had remained there so long, that the bags were found covered with a calcareous incrustation of considerable thickness; which being broken open with irons, the silver dollars showered out in great profusion." In addition to the silver thus "brought into the light of the sun, when it had been rusting under the waters for more than half a century," they discovered "vast treasures of gold, and pearls, and jewels"—in short, all that a Spanish galleon used formerly to be enriched with.

Captain Phipps and his company were not alone benefited by the discovery they had made. "In the course of the search, they were joined by one Adderley, a shipmaster from Providence, who had been of some assistance to Phipps in his former voyage, and who now met him by appointment in a small vessel. With his few hands, Adderley contrived, in a day or two, to load his vessel with silver, to the amount of several thousand pounds."

The failure of provisions obliged the whole company to take their departure before the examination of the wreck was complete. The last day that the men worked, they raised not less than twenty solid ingots of silver. To secure the benefits of whatever might remain, Phipps imposed an oath of secresy upon Adderley and his men, and exacted from them a promise that they would content themselves with what they had already received. But oaths and promises are of little account with such men. The secret was not kept, others visited the spot, and when Phipps returned, after the lapse of a year or two, it was found that every article of value had been taken away.

Captain Phipps' good fortune, (as he doubtless considered it, and as it proved in the end,) was the means of bringing him into immediate trouble with his men. They had, of choice, enlisted for *wages*, not wishing to incur any risk as to the issue of the voyage. And though they were less grasping and mutinous than his former crew, yet when they saw the vast amount of treasure which their vessel contained, the temptation was too great for them. Their plan was to divide the booty among themselves, and then " be gone to lead a short and merry life in some land, where the arrest of their employers would not be able to reach them."

In this solemn crisis of his affairs, Captain Phipps seems to have felt more deeply his need of Divine help, and to have been more impressed with religious considerations, than ever before.

"He made his vows," says Mather, "unto Almighty God, that if he would carry him safe home to England, with the treasures he had now given him, he would forever devote himself unto the interests of the Lord Jesus Christ, and of his people, more especially in that land which gave him birth." At the same time, he used all imaginable obliging arts to make his men true to him, assuring them, that, in addition to their wages, ample requitals should be made to them; and that, if the proprietors at home would not agree to this, he would divide his own share with them. Relying on his word, and won by his kindness, the crew now declared themselves content. Still, keeping a most watchful eye upon them, he thought it prudent to hasten back to England, not daring to stop so much as to take in provisions at any nearer port. He arrived safe in London, with all his treasure, in the year 1687.

The first thing now was, to make an equitable division of the profits; and here the integrity and generosity of the commander were conspicuous. According to the conditions of the patent, the government was entitled to a tenth. The men, also, received the gratuity which had been promised them, to their entire satisfaction. The remainder was so divided among the individuals interested, that Phipps' share amounted to only about sixteen thousand pounds. In addition to this, however, and in token of satisfaction with his conduct, the Duke of Albemarle presented Madame Phipps with a golden cup, worth not less than a thousand pounds.

There were those about the court who advised King James to seize the whole cargo, alleging that there had been some deception in procuring the patent. But the king indignantly rejected such infamous counsels. "He avowed his entire satisfaction with the conduct of the enterprise, and declared that Phipps had displayed so much integrity and talent, that he should not henceforth want his countenance. In consequence of the service done by him in bringing so much treasure into the country, and as an earnest of future favors, he conferred on him the honor of knighthood, and requested him to remain in England, with the promise of employment" in the navy.

CHAPTER II.

Sir William Phipps interests himself for New England. Makes a profession of religion in Boston. Captures Port Royal and the Eastern provinces. Fails in an expedition against Canada. Is appointed Governor of Massachusetts. His reception in Boston.

WHEN Sir William Phipps,—for henceforward we must speak of him under a new title,—had honorably discharged his freight, and settled his affairs in London, he began to think of his late vow, in relation to service for his native land. It was true, indeed, that he regarded himself as having been ill-treated by some of his own countrymen; but this did not at all abate his desire, or his conscious obligations, to do them good.

The situation of affairs in New England was at this time deplorable. The original colonial charter of Massachusetts had been taken away; and this outrage had been followed by the appointment, as governor, of Sir Edmund Andros,—a man well qualified, by his imperious temper and grasping disposition, to execute the arbitrary designs of the English court. The governor's secretary, and chief counselor was Edward Randolph, the old and constant enemy of the colonists, who had done more to disoblige and injure them, than any other man in the world.

The government of these men continued between two and three years; and to our venerable fathers it was truly a reign of terror. To use one of Mather's significant comparisons, "The foxes were now made the administrators of justice to the poultry." The religious rights of our ancestors were grossly invaded. The liberty of the press was taken away. Their very titles to their freeholds were called in question. They were led seriously to consider whether their lives would be long secure. In their distress and alarm, they contrived to send the Rev. Increase Mather as their agent to England, to lay their case directly before the king, and to implore protection and relief. He arrived in London in the spring of 1688, where he met his old parishioner, Sir William Phipps, and in whom he found a zealous and an efficient helper. Indeed, the measure of countenance which Mr. Mather received from king James, is by some ascribed almost entirely to the influence of Phipps, who had now a high reputation at court, and was a personal favorite with the king.

The immediate object of both was, to obtain the restoration of the colonial charter, or to secure, in some way, the rights and privileges of the people; but this they found it impossible to accomplish. On one occasion, the king intimated to Sir William, that whatever request he might make, would be favorably received. The latter immediately solicited the restoration of chartered privileges to his native land; but the king replied: "Anything but that, Sir William; anything but that."

Unable to succeed in his primary object, Phipps determined, after consulting with Mr. Mather, to apply for the office of sheriff of New England, hoping in that way to supply the country with firm and upright juries, and thus bring some relief to its suffering inhabitants; more especially to those who were obliged to defend, in the courts, the titles to their landed estates. It was not without much difficulty, and some money, that he obtained this office; and when he arrived in Boston with his commission, he found it impossible to execute it. The tyrannical governor, and his more grasping secretary, were resolved not to be checked in their career of plunder, by any such influences as he could command. Instead of yielding to him, they would fain have arrested him; and on one occasion, went so far as to make an attempt upon his life. "He was like to have been assassinated," says Mather, "before his own door, and in face of the sun."

At the commencement of the following year, 1689, we find Sir William again in England. The revolution had now taken place, king James was in exile, and William and Mary were on the throne. The fallen monarch, through one of his adherents in London, now offered to recall Andros, and to bestow on Phipps the government of New England; but the latter had too much wisdom to accept the offer. He was satisfied that James' power was at an end, and had no doubt that the revolution in England would be followed by one equally summary and salutary on the other side of the water, and so, in fact, it came to pass. No sooner had the news of king James' overthrow reached New England, than the people rose as one man; took possession of a frigate which had been stationed in the harbor of Boston, with a view to overawe them; drove Andros and his counselors into the fort; and compelled them, in a few hours, to surrender at discretion. The old colonial governor, Mr. Bradstreet, was induced to return to office, the former magistrates were restored, and the entire machinery of government was put in operation, much as it had been previous to the abrogation of the charter. Never was revolution more complete or satisfactory; the whole having been accomplished without the shedding of a drop of blood. Two additional agents were immediately sent to England, through whom a report of these proceedings were transmitted to the king. He signified his approbation of what had been done, and a commission was issued, empowering the Massachusetts government to act under the provisions of the old charter, till the principles on which colonial affairs were in future to be administered, could be definitively settled. Thus the political state of New England, was, for the time, established on its original basis; and Mr. Mather and his colleagues, had no longer any occasion to apply for a redress of present grievances, but only for a confirmation of existing privileges,—a circumstance which much increased their prospect of ultimate success.

The presence of Sir William Phipps being no longer required in England, he improved the opportunity to return to Boston, where he arrived in the summer of 1689. And here he remained for the greater part of a year, in the enjoyment of a quiet home, and of religious privileges, under the ministry of his distinguished friend and pastor, the Rev. Cotton Mather. This opportunity he improved for accomplishing what he had long intended and desired, viz., the making of a public profession of religion. On the 23d of March, 1690, he received the rite of baptism, and became a member of the Old North Church in Boston.

In accordance with what was then the invariable practice of that church, he was required to present a written narrative of his religious exercises, and experience; and I extract the entire paper, not only on account of its intrinsic interest, but because it is supposed to be the only authentic production of Sir William's pen, which is now extant. The narrative was addressed to the pastor, Rev. Cotton Mather, and is as follows:

"The first of God's making me sensible of my sins was in the year 1674, by hearing your father preach concerning *the day of trouble near.* I did then begin to think what I should do to be saved, and did bewail my youthful days, which I had spent in vain. I did think that I would begin to mind the things of God. Being then some time under your father's ministry, much troubled with my burden, but thinking of that Scripture, "Come unto me all ye that labor and are heavy laden, and I will give you rest," I had some thoughts of drawing as near to the communion of the Lord Jesus as I could; but the ruin which the Indian wars brought on my affairs, and the entanglements which my following the seas laid upon me, hindered my pursuing the welfare of my own soul, as I ought to have done. At length God was pleased to smile on my outward concerns. The various providences both merciful and afflictive, which attended me in my travels, were sanctified unto me, to make me acknowledge God in all my ways. I have divers times been in danger of my life; and I have been brought to see that I owe my life to him who has given his precious life for me. I thank God, he hath brought me to see myself altogether unhappy without an interest in the Lord Jesus Christ, and to close heartily with him, desiring him to execute all his offices on my behalf. I have now, for some time, been under serious resolutions, that I would avoid whatever I should know to be displeasing to God, and that I would serve him, all the days of my life. I believe no man will repent the service of such a master. I find myself unable to keep such resolutions, but my serious prayers are to the Most High, that he would enable me. God hath done so much for me, that I am sensible I owe myself to him. To him I give myself, and all that he has given me. I cannot express his mercies to me. But as soon as ever God had smiled upon me with a turn of my affairs, I laid myself under solemn vows, that I would set myself to serve his people and churches here, to the utmost of my capacity. I have had great offers made me in England, but the churches of New England, were those which my heart was most set upon. I knew, that if God had a people anywhere, it was here; and I resolved to rise and fall with them; neglecting very great advantages for my worldly interest, that I might come and enjoy the ordinances of the Lord Jesus here.

"It has been my trouble, that since I came home, I have made no more haste to get into the *house of God*, where I desire to be; especially having heard so much about the evil of that omission. I can do little for God; but I desire to wait upon him in his ordinances, and to live to his honor and glory.

"My being born in a part of the country where I had not, in my infancy, enjoyed the first sacrament of the New Testament has been something of a stumbling block to me. But though I have had proffers of baptism elsewhere, I resolved rather to defer it, until I might enjoy it in the communion of these churches. I have also had awful impressions from those words of the Lord Jesus, 'Whosoever shall be ashamed of me, and of my words, of him shall the Son of Man be ashamed.'

"When God had blessed me with something of this world, I had no trouble so great as this, *lest it should not be in mercy;* and I trembled at nothing more than being put off with a portion here. That I may make sure of better things, I now offer myself unto the communion of this church of the Lord Jesus."

This document bears indubitable marks of the sincerity and true piety of its author. There is manifest in it a deep sense of the Divine goodness and of his own unworthiness on account of sin, a simple trust in the Lord Jesus Christ as the sinner's only hope, and an earnest consecration of the whole soul to him, which no hypocrite could well counterfeit. Indeed, hypocrisy, on any subject, could never be charged upon Sir William Phipps. He was a plain, blunt, outspoken man, whose faults lay on the side of frankness, sometimes hastiness of speech, rather than on the side of concealment.

The circumstances in which Sir William was now placed,—his ample fortune, his high standing and reputation, his quiet and comfortable home, would have satisfied most other men, and disposed them to a retired and domestic life.

But such a life had no charms for him, nor indeed could he reconcile it with his convictions of duty. In conversation with his pastor, he frequently expressed his feelings on this wise: "I have no need to look after any farther advantages for myself in this world; I may sit still at home, if I will, and enjoy my ease for the rest of my life; but I believe that I should offend God in so doing: For I am now in the prime of my age and strength, and I thank God, I can endure hardship. He only knows how long I have to live. But I think it is my duty to venture my life in doing good, before a useless old age comes upon me. Wherefore, I will now expose myself where I am able, and as far as I am able, for the service of my country. I was born for others, as well as for myself."

There is no reason to question the sincerity of this language; and certainly it indicates a noble and generous mind. It expresses the feelings both of the patriot and the Christian. And circumstances immediately occurred,—indeed, they were already occurring, which put his patriotism to the test.

The French were at this time in possession of nearly all of what is now termed British America, on the North and East of us, and of Louisiana on the West. Between them and the

English colonies on every side, were widely extended and almost unbroken forests,—the possession and the abode of various tribes of Indians. With these Indians, our forefathers might, in general, have maintained peace, could they only have been kept from foreign influence; but French priests and emissaries, who were among them, were continually instigating them to violate their treaties with the English, and to fall upon and plunder their defenceless villages. Such was the origin of nearly all the Indian wars of that day; more especially those in New Hampshire and Maine. The policy of the French was, to drive out, and destroy the English colonists; to take possession of their towns and settlements; to supplant the Protestant religion by the Romish; and to divide with Spain the whole American continent.

At this very time a destructive Indian war was raging on the frontiers, and had been so for several months. Schenectady, in New York, Salmon Falls, in New Hampshire, and Fort Pemaquid, in Maine, had successively fallen into the hands of the enemy. The Indians had possession of all the eastern and central parts of Maine, and were pushing their conquests into the older settlements. Experience had shown that it was to little purpose to make treaties with these savages; so long as the French continued to supply them with arms and ammunition, and to encourage them in their wars, they would not regard any engagements into which they might enter, but would continue their work of plunder and death.

A plan was matured, therefore, (of which Sir William Phipps was in part the contriver, as he was the leader,) to take forcible possession of some of the principal French fortresses and towns, and ultimately to drive them from this part of North America.

Port Royal was then the capital of the French province of Acadia, (now Nova Scotia,) and was defended by a fort. It was conveniently situated for furnishing supplies to the eastern Indians, and for affording a shelter to the privateers which plundered the English shipping, and occasionally the smaller settlements on the coast. In short, it was one of the rallying points from which issued forth most of the bad influences with which our fathers, at that period, were obliged to contend. It was determined, therefore, by means of a naval armament, to attempt the capture of Port Royal; and Sir William Phipps, though not accustomed to military operations, was constituted the commander of the enterprise.

In his instructions, which were furnished him by Governor Bradstreet, he was ordered "to take care that the worship of God be maintained and duly observed on board all the vessels; to offer the enemy fair terms upon summons, to which, if they accede, the said terms are to be faithfully observed; but if not, you are to gain the best advantage you may—to assault, kill, and utterly extirpate the common enemy, and to burn and demolish their fortifications and shipping. Having reduced Port Royal, you are to proceed along the coast, for the reducing of the other places and plantations, in the possession of the French, unto obedience to the crown of England."

Furnished with these instructions, Sir William sailed from Nantasket on the 28th of April, 1690, with a fleet of seven or eight vessels, and an army of about seven hundred men. He arrived at Port Royal on the 11th of May. The French governor, Meneval, was taken completely by surprise; nor was the town, though containing several thousand inhabitants, in a situation to afford any effectual resistance. The conquest, therefore, was short and easy. "Sir William took possession of the place, in the name of the English government, demolished the fort, and administered the oath of allegiance to those of the French inhabitants who chose to remain.

He then appointed a governor of the town, with a small garrison, and set sail on his return, carrying with him a large amount of property. On his way home, he landed at the various settlements, and took formal possession of the coast, from Port Royal to Penobscot. The whole province of Acadia was thus subdued, and remained in the possession of the English till the peace of Ryswick, in 1697, when it was restored to the French."

On the return of the armament, a committee was appointed "to take charge of the property brought from Port Royal; to sell the same; and from the proceeds, to defray the expenses of the expedition. Should there be any surplus, the same is to be divided into two equal parts; the one to be reserved for the use of the colony, and the other to be applied for the use of the officers and soldiers who have been engaged in the service." The surplus thus divided is supposed to have been considerable.

During the absence of Phipps, the Indians, under the direction of the Canadians, "had been carrying on the war with much success in Maine. In the early part of May, the fort at Casco was surprised, and more than a hundred men were taken prisoners. The loss of this post compelled the weaker garrisons along the coast to fall back upon Saco, and ultimately upon Wells, leaving the whole eastern country either in actual possession of the enemy, or entirely defenceless." The news of these disasters caused much alarm at Boston, and led our forefathers to the determination, if possible, to get possession of Quebec and the Canadas, as they were already in possession of Port Royal and the eastern provinces.

This enterprise had been talked of before the return of Phipps and his squadron; but when his successes came to be known, it assumed a new interest, and was resolved on without delay. Every encouragement was given to induce volunteers to enlist for the service, and the most strenuous efforts were made to procure the requisite amount of funds. Letters were dispatched to England, setting forth the great importance of the undertaking, and asking assistance, more especially in the supply of ammunition and arms. Sir William Phipps was constituted first in command, and Major John Walley, second; and by the middle of July, a fleet, consisting of thirty-two vessels, having on board some 2200 men, was in readiness to depart. An arrangement had been made with the governors of New York and Connecticut, by which a land expedition from these colonies was to invest Montreal, at the same time that Phipp's armament appeared before Quebec.

Perhaps no warlike expedition in the early history of our country was ever more wisely planned than this. Nor had there ever been one, in regard to which public expectation was more raised and intense. And certainly no one, either before or since, ever proved a more decided failure, and all this without seriously implicating either the skill or the bravery of the commander. The principal causes of the failure were the following:

In the first place, the expedition was delayed, waiting for supplies from England (which never came) till the proper season for commencing it, for that year, was past. Then there was a further delay, from contrary winds, from the difficulty of procuring pilots, and from the necessity, at the last, of proceeding without them. Besides, the promised co-operation from New York and Connecticut was not realized. Their troops, after commencing their march, became disheartened and turned back, leaving the entire French force in Canada, which otherwise would have been divided, to concentrate itself at Quebec. In addition to all this, a malignant fever and the small-pox broke out in the fleet, and made painful ravages among the troops.

Notwithstanding all these hindrances and discouragements, Sir William persevered, and on the 5th of October appeared before Quebec. The next day he sent an officer on shore, with a summons to the governor to surrender; which summons was haughtily and indignantly answered. As soon as it could be done, about thirteen hundred of the troops—all who were ablè, and could be spared from the ships—were landed under the direction of Major Walley; but they had to encounter the most formidable difficulties from cold and storm, from the unanticipated number and force of the enemy, and more especially from the cowardice and incompetency of their leader. This last circumstance was a sufficient cause of their defeat, if there had been no other. Sir William, with some his larger ships, sailed up the river and bombarded the town; but the houses being built mostly of stone, with sides too thick for a ball to penetrate, the firing caused but little injury.

The army remained on shore some three or four days, defending themselves as best they could against the combined force of the elements, and the bullets of the French and Indians, but making no effective advances towards the capture of the place. At length, there seemed to be no alternative but to return to their ships; and the expedition was reluctantly abandoned.

The return of the fleet, at that inclement season of the year, was peculiarly disastrous. Owing to violent storms, it was found impossible to keep the ships together. One vessel was never heard of after they separated. Another was burnt at sea. Four of them were blown so far from the coast, that they did not reach Boston for several weeks after the rest of the fleet, when they had been given up as lost. The fate of one was so very peculiar as to require a more particular description. It was commanded by Capt. John Rainsford, contained sixty men, and was wrecked, on the night of the 28th of October, on a desolate island, in the gulf of St. Lawrence. For several days, the crew hoped to get off; but despairing of this at last, they went ashore with their provisions, and made such preparations as they could for spending the cold, long winter on the island. They built "nine small chimney-less things, which they called houses," and also a shelter for their stores. Having not more than a supply of pro visions for a month, and expecting to remain on the island six or seven months, they were obliged to put themselves upon the shortest allowance possible. They established laws for their little community; maintained the daily worship of God in their houses; and "observed the Lord's day with more solemn exercises of religion."

Before the middle of winter, more than half of their number had died. In addition to the rest of their troubles, they had those among them who would not be satisfied with the daily allowance of provisions, but were continually pilfering from the common stock. In particular, says Mather, "there was a wicked Irishman, who had such a voracious devil within him, that after divers burglaries upon the storehouse, he at last stole and eat with such a pamphagous fury, as to cram himself with no less than eighteen stolen biscuits at one meal; and he was fain to have his belly rubbed and bathed before the fire, lest he should have burst." As a measure of necessity, in order to their own preservation, the company had serious thoughts of putting this wretch to death; but it does not appear that they did so.

These men continued together till the 25th of March, when five of their number took a boat which had been saved from their vessel, and committed themselves to the waves, with the intention, if possible, of getting to Boston, and then of returning for the rest of the crew. In this open boat, exposed to storms, winds, icebergs, and all sorts of perils, these five men were confined no less than forty-five days; when, on the ninth of May, they actually came into Boston, greatly to the surprise and joy of their friends, who had put on mourning for them as dead. A vessel was immediately sent to the relief of the survivors, which brought them in safety to their homes.

As remarked already, the defeat of this Canadian enterprise can in no way be attributed to want of capacity or courage on the part of the commander-in-chief; nor was it so considered by our fathers at the time. It seems to have been peculiarly the work of Providence, and that, too, a mysterious Providence. In view of it, Sir William Phipps said, "that though he had been used to *diving* in his day," (alluding to the manner in which he had recovered so much treasure from the ocean,) "the things which had befallen him in this expedition were *too deep to be dived into.*" For had only one of three or four contingencies been ordered differently, the result might have been as happy as it was now disastrous. If, for example, the troops from New York and Connecticut had fulfilled their engagements in attacking Montreal, or if mortal sickness had not invaded the fleet, and destroyed or disabled great numbers of the soldiers, or if the second officer in command, who had the entire direction of the land forces, had exhibited the same capacity and bravery as the leader—more especially, if the expedition had not been delayed by contrary winds and storms, giving the enemy opportunity to concentrate his forces and strengthen his fortifications—in all probability Quebec might have been easily taken. Indeed, La Hontan, a French writer who was on the spot, affirms, that had Sir William arrived before Quebec only one week earlier, he might have taken it without striking a blow; as there were then but two hundred regular troops in the place, which was open and exposed in every direction.

The disastrous failure of this expedition threw the government of the colony into great embarrassment. The people were distressed, not only by the loss of property and of friends, but by an onerous public debt, which they had not the ability to pay. It was at this time, and under these circumstances, that the first experiment was made in this country of *paper money*. "Bills of credit were issued, which the faith of the government was pledged to redeem. The notes were of various denominations, from two shillings up to ten pounds sterling; and as no greater amount was issued than would be brought into the treasury in two years by taxes, and as express provision was made that these notes should be received, even at five per cent. advance, in payment of taxes, it was hoped that the paper would circulate, as of equal value with gold or silver." And so in fact it would, had the government of the country been in a more settled state. But as the existing government was merely a provisional one, which might be abolished or changed at any time by the king, it was thought that the faith of the government was not a sufficient security.

Numerous expedients were resorted to, to keep up the credit of these notes. To this end, Sir William Phipps set a noble example, in consenting to receive a large amount of them, at par, in exchange for gold and silver. Still, the credit of the bills fell, so that the holders of them did not receive, in some instances, more than fourteen shillings to the pound. They were all redeemed, ultimately, by the government at their full value; but the holders of them, at the time of redemption, were in general capitalists, and not the poor soldiers, who ought in justice to have received the benefit.

But it is time that we return to Sir William Phipps. He arrived in Boston, with the remains of his fleet, on the 19th of November; defeated indeed as to the grand object of his Canadian expedition, but still not in despair as to final success. In fact, the word *despair* seems to have had no place in his vocabulary, as the thing itself had no place in his heart. He immediately resolved upon a voyage to England, with a view to lay before the king in person, "the considerations in favor of another attempt to wrest from the French all their North American possessions." He accordingly embarked in the depth of winter, and after a tedious passage arrived at Bristol, whence he hastened on to London.

"He there offered the king his services in the command of a second expedition; and in a paper which he presented, strongly set forth the importance and feasibility of the scheme." The reasons which he urged were, in substance, as follows: 1, The success of the design would give the English the exclusive benefit of the fur trade, and secure from further injury the Hudson's Bay Company, several of whose factories had recently fallen into the hands of the enemy. 2, It would also secure the Newfoundland fisheries, and materially increase the amount of that business. 3, It would afford the greatest encouragement, and might be necessary even to the existence of the American colonies. For, if the French were allowed to retain their possessions in the country, the constantly increasing influence of the priests would finally enlist all the Indians on their side, and by this means the English might be at length extirpated.

These were all sound arguments, but the English government was not then in a situation to undertake the enterprise. After the lapse of another half century, it *was* undertaken and carried through; although at an expense of blood and treasure an hundred-fold greater than would have been necessary, had the representations of Phipps and the colonists been listened to at the proper time.

But though Sir William failed of the *immediate* object which led him to England, the event proved that Divine providence had sent him there for another object. The Rev. Mr. Mather and his associates were still there, endeavoring to procure the restoration of the former colonial charter. But this was found to be impracticable. The question then was, whether to accept a new charter, such as they might be able to secure, or to return without any, trusting to the king's clemency to continue the existing provisional government. On this question, the agents of the colony were divided among themselves; Mr. Mather and Sir Henry Ashurst being in favor of a charter, and the other members of the agency opposing it. Sir William Phipps arrived in London just at the time when this question was agitated, and united his influence with that of Mr. Mather. The colony had suffered so much under the late king, that they were unwilling to trust the mere word of a king any further. And this was understood to be the sentiment of a majority of their constituents at home.

Henceforward, therefore, the efforts of the agents were chiefly directed to the negotiating and procuring of a new charter. In this, they were essentially aided by Sir William Phipps. Nor did they fail to enlist the good offices of the queen, who consented to write to the king in Holland on their behalf.

About the first of September, the instrument was completed; and Mr. Mather was desired to nominate a candidate for the office of governor. On this question his mind had long been made up. The fact that Sir William Phipps was a native of New England, that he possessed a high rank and a large estate, that he had already served the crown in several important capacities, and had obtained the favor of the king without forfeiting his popularity at home,—these several considerations clearly pointed him out as by far the most suitable person for the office. His name was accordingly presented to the council; and when Mr. Mather, a few days afterwards, obtained an audience of the king, he addressed him in the following terms: "In the behalf of New England, I do most humbly thank your majesty, that you have been pleased, by a charter, to restore English liberty unto your subjects in that country, to confirm them in their property, and to grant them some peculiar privileges. I doubt not but that they will demean themselves with such dutiful affection and loyalty to your majesty, that you will see cause to enlarge your favors towards them. And I do most humbly thank your majesty, in that you have been pleased to give leave unto those that are concerned for New England to nominate their governor. Sir William Phipps has accordingly been nominated at the council board. He hath done a good service for the crown, by enlarging your dominions, and reducing Nova Scotia to your obedience. I know that he will faithfully serve your majesty, to the utmost of his capacity; and if your majesty shall think fit to confirm him in that place, it will be a further obligation on your subjects there."

In consequence of this nomination, a commission was prepared, under the great seal, by which Sir William Phipps was appointed Captain-general and Governor-in-chief of the Province of Massachusetts Bay in New England. Under this title were included, by the new charter, not only the old colony of Massachusetts, but also the Plymouth colony, the Provinces of Maine and Nova Scotia, and all the country lying between them, as far north as the St. Lawrence river. By his commission, he was also constituted Captain-general of the colonies of Connecticut and Rhode Island.

Sir William, with Mr. Mather, was admitted to kiss the king's hand, on the third of January, 1692. Early in the spring they embarked in the None-Such frigate for New England, and arrived at Boston in May of the same year. The General Court were soon called together, when they passed a resolve, appointing a day of solemn thanksgiving to Almighty God, "for granting a safe arrival to his excellency, the governor, and the Rev. Mr. Increase Mather, who have industriously endeavored the service of this people, and have brought over with them a settlement of government, in which their majesties have graciously given us distinguishing marks of the royal favor and goodness."

On the Monday following his arrival, Gov. Phipps was inaugurated. The ceremonies and services of the occasion were as follows: He was conducted from his own house to the town-house by a large military escort, and by the principal gentlemen of Boston and vicinity. The services were opened with prayer by Rev. Mr. Allen, one of the ministers of Boston. The charter was next read; then the governor's commission; after which the venerable governor Bradstreet resigned the chair. The commission of Lieutenant-governor Stoughton was also read. The whole was concluded with a public dinner from which the governor was escorted back to his house.

CHAPTER III.

Governor Phipps' administration. His measures for the suppression of witchcraft. His dealings with the Indians. Encounters opposition and enemies. Is summoned to England. His sudden death. His general character.

As Sir William Phipps was the first governor under the new charter, it may well be supposed that, at his very entrance upon office, many things would require attention. Magistrates were to be appointed, laws to be framed, and the entire government to be organized and put in operation, according to the provisions of the new constitution. In all these important matters, the governor demeaned himself as a true son of New England. The spirit which he manifested was kind and conciliatory, willing to forego the full exercise of his prerogative, and to consult the wishes of those for whom he ruled. Thus, at the first meeting of the council for the appointment of civil officers, instead of nominating them himself, as he might have done, he permitted them to be nominated by the members present, himself only voting on the question of their approval. To the representatives, also, he was accustomed to use language such as this: "Gentlemen, you may make yourselves as easy as you will. Consider what may have any tendency to your welfare, and be sure that whatever bills you offer me, consistent with the honor and interest of the crown, I shall pass them readily. I do but seek opportunities to serve you. Had it not been for this, I should never have accepted the government of the Province. And whenever you have settled such a body of good laws, that no person coming after me may make you uneasy, I shall not desire one day longer to continue in the government." In accordance with these declarations, says Mather, the governor "passed every act for the welfare of the province which was proposed to him; and instead of ever putting them upon buying his assent to any good act," (as more than one of the royal governors afterwards did) "he was much more forward to give it, than they were to ask it."

Sir William Phipps entered upon his government in the very midst of the excitement respecting witchcraft. At the time of his arrival, Justices Corwin and Hathorne had been for months holding their witch courts at Salem, and the jails were filled with suspected or indicted persons. What the governor's particular views of the subject were, we have no means of knowing. The probability is, that he had never given much attention to it, and that he fell in with the prevailing opinions. But whether he did so, or not, it was necessary for him, as chief magistrate, to take some decisive action in regard to it; and I know not whether, under existing circumstances, he could have pursued a more satisfactory course than he did.

With the advice and consent of council, a commission was issued to seven of the principal citizens and jurists of the colony, viz.: Lieut. Governor Stoughton, Maj. Saltonstall, Maj. Richards, Maj. Gedney, Mr. Wait Winthrop, Capt. Sewall, and Mr. Sergeant, constituting them a court, to try the accused persons at Salem. The judges first assembled, June 2d, and tried and condemned one, who was executed on the tenth. The court then adjourned to June 30th; and in the meantime, the governor and council asked advice of the ministers of Boston and the vicinity, as to the course to be pursued. After due deliberation, the ministers gave their advice, under the following particulars:

1. They express their sympathy with those who are "suffering by molestation from the invisible world," and "think that their condition calls for the utmost help of all persons, in their several capacities."

2. They thankfully acknowledged the success which has followed the efforts of the magistrates "to defeat the withcrafts," and pray for a full and perfect discovery of all this mysterious wickedness.

3. They recommend "a very critical and exquisite caution, lest, by too much credulity for things received only upon the devil's authority, there be a door opened for a long train of miserable consequences."

4. The rulers are exhorted not to proceed, in any case, upon mere presumption, and to show "an exceeding tenderness towards those that may be complained of, especially if they have been persons of an unblemished reputation."

5. The next advice is, that the primary examination of suspected persons may be without noise, company or excitement, and that there "may be nothing used as a test for the trial of the suspected, the lawfulness whereof may be doubted by the people of God."

6. The ministers recommend to the magis-

trates not to convict, or so much as commit persons, on what was called "the spectral evidence;" inasmuch as it is an undoubted thing that a demon may appear, even to ill purposes, in the shape of an innocent and virtuous man. They also pronounce any "alteration made in the sufferers by a look or touch of the accused," to be insufficient evidence of guilt.

7. The ministers further suggest, whether "another rejection of the testimonies commonly relied on, whose whole force and strength is from the devils alone, may not put a period unto the progress of the terrible calamity begun upon us, in the accusation of so many persons, whereof some, we hope, are clear of the great transgression laid to their charge."

8. Having given the above directions, suggestions and cautions, the ministers "humbly recommend to the government the speedy and vigorous prosecution of such as have rendered themselves obnoxious, according to the directions given in the laws of God, and the wholesome statutes of the English nation."*

By those who seem inclined to traduce the ministers of that day, (and more especially Cot-

* This paper of advices may be found entire, in Hutchinson's Hist. of Mass., Vol. II., p. 52.

ton Mather, by whom these advices are said to have been drawn up,) this *last* article is almost the only one quoted or referred to. It is quoted often, as though it stood alone, without any restriction or qualification; as if the ministers were only anxious to have the judges make all due despatch, and condemn and hang the suspected witches as fast as possible. But this, it will be seen, is altogether an unjust view of the case. These advices of the ministers are to be taken and judged of, as a *whole;* and as a whole, they were manifestly framed and designed with a view to reprove much of the previous proceeding, particularly that of the Salem justices, and to prevent, so far as possible, the like proceedings in future. They do, indeed, "recommend the speedy and vigorous prosecution of those who have *justly* rendered themselves obnoxious;" but the recommendation is accompanied with such *cautions*, *restrictions*, and *qualifications*, that, had they been duly regarded, there probably had not been another individual convicted. If the trials had been conducted with that "exceeding tenderness" towards the accused, which the ministers recommended; if the "spectral evidence," together with all improper tests, had been set aside; if all testimony of every kind, which rested only on the devil's authority, had been rejected, the judges might have proceeded as vigorously as they pleased,—the more vigorously the better; for by this means the jails had been the sooner emptied, and the accused persons had been set at liberty.

From persons who believed in the reality of witchcraft, and that the proper witch is deserving of death, (as all these ministers most seriously did,) I see not how better advice than that which they proffered to the magistrates on this occasion, could reasonably have been expected. And happy had it been for all concerned, if the judges had been content to follow it. But they would not. At least, some of them would not, particularly chief justice Stoughton. He seems to have been fully satisfied, at least for a time, as to the validity of the "spectral evidence," and other branches of the devil's testimony; and consequently the work of hanging went on.

The court had several sessions during the summer, and nineteen persons in all were executed. Happily, the trials were adjourned from September to January; in which time opportunity was furnished for consideration, and for the delusion more fully to develope itself; and when the court came together again, nearly all who were put upon trial were acquitted, and those who were not put on trial were, by order of the governor, discharged. "Such a jail delivery," says Hutchinson, "was made at this court, as was never known at any other time in New England."

The conduct of Governor Phipps was such, at this trying period, as to procure for him not only the thanks of his own countrymen, but the favorable notice of the Queen. "She did him the honor," says Mather, "to write unto him very gracious letters, wherein her Majesty commended his proceedings in these mysterious matters."

A story is told of lady Phipps, in this connection, which is quite too good to be omitted. During her husband's absence, her interposition was requested in behalf of a woman, who had been committed by one of the justices on a charge of witchcraft, by a formal warrant, under his hand and seal. The poor woman was in close confinement, expecting her trial at the next assize, which was near at hand. Madam Phipps believed the case to be one in which the forms of law might well be dispensed with. She signed a warrant with her own hand for the woman's discharge, which order was obeyed by the keeper, and the woman was set at liberty. It was not long after this, that lady Phipps herself was suspected, if not accused, of witchcraft.

The history of this delusion is not one to be merely deplored, or laughed at. It is an instructive history, and particularly so at the present day. *We* live in an age of marvels, some of them claiming to be well attested, and challenging the belief of the community. But if we compare the wonders of this age with those of Salem and the vicinity, in 1692, we shall find that the latter have even stronger evidence in their favor, than the former. The latter were attested, in some instances, by hundreds of witnesses, and were recorded by grave men on the page of history. And now, if any one asks whether I believe the witch stories of 1692, I answer, that I as much believe them, as I do that sleep-walkers in our day visit the moon and the planets, hold converse with their inhabitants, receive letters from the spiritual world, and perform other feats equally strange and unaccountable. The evidence in favor of the witch stories is greater, I repeat, than that for the marvels of our own times; and the faith of those who have full confidence in the latter, ought not to misgive or stagger at the former.

But to return from this digression. The delusion under which our fathers labored respecting witchcraft, was as short-lived, as it was violent. The people were soon awakened by a sense of their common danger; and though a few individuals here and there, continued to urge prosecutions, the juries refused to convict. And one of the last public acts of Sir William Phipps was to issue a general pardon to all who had been convicted or accused of the offence.

At an early period in his administration, the new Governor was called to contend with a class of enemies more tangible, if not more formidable, than witches and demons. An Indian war had broken out again on the Eastern frontier, and was raging in different parts of Maine. To restore confidence to the settlers, and to afford the best means of restraining and repelling the enemy, it was determined to erect a strong fortress, at some central point along the coast. The site selected for this purpose was on the Pemaquid river, near the mouth, at the Southern extremity of what is now Bristol, Maine. A fort had previously existed there, which the Indians had destroyed; but a more permanent one was now to be erected. For this purpose the Governor, attended by

Major Church and four hundred and fifty men, embarked at Boston, in August, 1692, and shortly after arrived at Pamaquid. The fort was in a quadrangular form, and the walls were of stone. It was named Fort William Henry; and was of great service both to the settlers and the government. The war with the Indians was now pursued with so much vigor, that in the course of a few months, they were inclined to peace. A treaty was formed and signed at Pemaquid, in August of the following year.

While the peace continued, Governor Phipps took all proper measures to conciliate the good will of the Indians, and induce them to break off their connection with the French. For this purpose, he made several voyages from Boston to Pemaquid, and had repeated interviews with their principal chiefs. On one occasion, he took an Indian preacher with him, for the purpose of instructing them in Protestant Christianity. But the artifices of the Jesuits were as various as they were contemptible, and their influence, in the end, proved too strong for him. The chiefs would receive the Governor's presents, and make fair promises; but on the first favorable opportunity, would renew their depredations.

As a specimen of the kind of instruction which the Catholic priests of that day afforded the Indians, I may notice the following: The Indians were taught, says Mather, that the blessed virgin, the mother of our Saviour, was a *French lady;* and that the soldiers who crucified him were *Englishmen.* Hence, to destroy an Englishman was regarded by them as a meritorious service.

Governor Phipps' administration was short; and though one of great service to the country, it was not altogether peaceful or pleasant to himself. That party in the Province who were averse to the new charter, would naturally oppose the man by whose influence, in a considerable degree, the charter was procured, and who was the first to administer the government under it. These men were the persevering, unrelenting *demagogues* of the times; and they lost no opportunity of thwarting the Governor's measures, impugning his motives, and resisting his authority and influence.

In connection with these, there was a clique of selfish, interested individuals at the English court. More especially, the infamous Joseph Dudley was there, intriguing and plotting against the Governor, that he might effect his removal, and have his place. Dudley had been a principal counselor and minister of Sir Edmund Andros, and by this means had made himself so odious in New England, that he was obliged to flee his country. But he was now scheming and planning to return, and that, too, not as a private citizen, but as the chief magistrate;—a design, which, after a while, he accomplished, much to the discomfort of all good men.

But Governor Phipps' troubles arose, not alone from the machinations of his enemies, but in part, (for the truth must be told) from his own *indiscretions.* He had been bred a sailor, not a governor; and his habits were better adapted to the control of a literal ship, than to the direction of the ship of state. His heart was kind and generous—this no one could doubt; but his temper was hasty, and unused to restraint, and this led him, in a few instances, to say and do things which were not becoming the dignity of his station.

His first quarrel was with one Brenton, collector of the port of Boston, who refused to obey his orders, and whom he chastised with his own hands. He had a similar difficulty with Captain Short, of the None-Such Frigate, which was stationed at the time at Boston. The Governor had ordered Short to sail for St. John's, to intercept a French man-of-war which was expected there. Short reluctantly obeyed the order, and proceeded on his voyage, but with so much hesitation and delay, that the Frenchman escaped out of his hands. The Governor meeting him in the street soon after his return, accused him of negligence and cowardice, and (after some hard words on both sides) used his cane over his head.

Such methods of discipline in a New England Governor, however great may have been his provocation, were certainly undignified and unjustifiable, and his enemies did not fail to make the most of them. Both Brenton and Short soon made their appearance in England, where they preferred complaints against him, and united with Dudley and others in requesting that he might be displaced. The king, however, would not recall or censure him before he was heard, and sent him an order to come to England and make his defence. Accordingly, he left Boston in the month of November, 1694, carrying with him an address from the house of representatives, praying that the Governor might not be removed.

On his arrival in London, he was arrested by

Dudley and Brenton, in actions of twenty thousand pounds damages. This proceeding on the part of Dudley seems to have been one of pure spite. He had received no injury from the Governor, and his design could only have been to embarrass his situation, and perhaps to ingratiate himself with the opposition at home.

These actions, however, seem to have given his Excellency no great trouble; nor indeed had he any difficulty in so far vindicating himself to his Sovereign, as to have (to use the language of Mather,) "all human assurance" of being permitted, in a few weeks, to return to his government.

Accordingly, he seems to have dismissed, almost entirely, his own personal affairs, and to have occupied himself, during his stay in London, with various designs for the public good. One was, a plan "for supplying the English navy with timber and naval stores from the Eastern parts of New England. The conception," says Mr. Bowen, "was plausible, and no person was better fitted than himself to carry it into execution."

Another thing which he had in mind, and of which, for years, he had never lost sight, was the reduction of Canada. Hitherto, Divine providence had defeated all his endeavors for the accomplishment of this important object; and the present moment seemed a favorable one to urge it personally upon the English government, and to concert measures for carrying it into effect.

He had still another plan which he was intending to accomplish, even if it required the resignation of his government. He knew that the ship, having on board the Spanish Governor Bobadilla, together with a vast amount of gold and silver, had been cast away somewhere in the West Indies, and he supposed that he had gained such information as would enable him to discover the wreck. He was proposing, therefore, to secure a patent in his own name, and to make one more attempt to possess himself of the treasures of the deep.

But the designs of his fertile and busy brain were all suddenly arrested by mortal sickness. He took a violent cold, in the month of February, 1695, which resulted in a malignant fever, and this, in a few days, carried him to his grave. He died in the 45th year of his age, and was honorably interred in the church of St. Mary Woolnoth, London.

Sir William Phipps left no children. His

estate was chiefly inherited by the Hon. Spencer Phipps, a nephew whom he had adopted into his family, and whose name frequently occurs in the history of the colony. His widow afterwards married a Mr. Sergeant, who was a member of the Board of Council in the year 1702.

I have already said, that Sir William Phipps was a man of great stature. Mather says, that "he was thick as well as tall, and strong as well as thick; able to conquer such difficulties of diet and travel, as would have killed most men alive." He is said to have been of a comely, manly countenance, indicating (what he certainly possessed) a generous mind.

His residence in Boston was at the head of what was, originally, "Green Lane." Out of compliment to him, and to commemorate his agency in procuring the provincial charter, this Lane was afterwards called "Charter Street." The house remained standing, at the corner of Charter and Salem Streets, until within a few years, when it was pulled down to make way for modern improvements.

The faults of Sir William Phipps were chiefly such as sprung from his want of early education, and from his habits and associates in middle life. That he had *many virtues*, in reference to which he may safely be held up as an example, all respectable authorities agree.

His most prominent characteristics were those at which I hinted in the commencement of this memoir, viz., enterprise, energy, and persevering industry. It was these, rather than *good luck*, as it is sometimes called—rather than any *unsought*, *unlooked for interpositions*, which raised him from poverty to affluence, and from the humblest walks of life to that high and honorable station which he finally occupied.

But these properties alone could never have thus exalted him. He might have had all these, and if he had lacked honor, honesty, and strict Puritan integrity, he had only been the more accomplished villain. He would have the sooner involved himself in infamy and ruin. In all his eventful history, Sir William Phipps is not known to have been chargeable with one mean, dishonest, or dishonorable transaction.* He

---

* The only exception to this statement, of which I have any knowledge, relates to his conduct at the taking of Port Royal. It has been said, that the town was not captured, but *surrendered;* and that, according to the terms of capitulation, *private property was to be respected.* In reply to this, I need only say, that there is no evidence, aside from the word of Meneval, the French governor, that *there was any stipulation in regard to private property.* And

violated no contracts. He would not raise expectation only to disappoint it, or encourage confidence to betray it. He would descend to no base, hypocritical artifices to supplant a rival, or to rid himself of burthensome obligations. His faults, as I before stated, all lay in the opposite direction. He was, through life, a frank, honest, open-hearted, out-spoken man; and these were the traits of character which inspired public confidence, and retained it. It was these traits, in common with those to which I before referred, which changed the untutored shepherd boy into the skillful artisan, the bold ship-master, the successful military chieftain, the Provincial Governor;—which made him, in short, what for a time he certainly was, *the first man in his country.*

The Rev. Dr. Mather, who was his intimate

---

if there was none, the habitual rapacity of the French and Indians fully justified Phipps, at least according to the notions of that age, in all that he did. There *were* stipulations in regard to the disposal of the prisoners, and these were satisfactorily complied with. It is remarkable that good old governor Bradstreet, and his council, make no complaint of Capt. Phipps, in relation to this matter. Indeed, if he erred, they were *participes criminæ*, partners of his guilt. They shared the spoils, and expected to, if any were acquired. It is remarkable, too, that Hutchinson utters not a note of censure on the subject. The presumption, therefore, is, that no stipulation was entered into, which was not fulfilled.

friend and pastor, has mentioned several other traits of character, in which Sir William Phipps was worthy of all imitation. One of these was a *forgiving spirit.* "I never saw three men in the world," says he, "who equalled him in this respect. In the vast variety of business through which he *raced* in his time, he met with many and mighty injuries; but although I have heard all that the most venomous malice could hiss at his memory, I never did hear, unto this hour, that he ever once *deliberately* revenged an injury.* Under great provocations, he would commonly say, 'It is no matter; let them alone. Some time or other they will see their weakness and rashness, and have occasion for me to do them a kindness; and then they will see that I have quite forgotten all their baseness.'"

It is not uncommon for persons, when suddenly raised from humble life to the possession of great wealth and honors, to become purse-proud, imperious, and overbearing. But nothing of this was observable in the case of Sir William Phipps. On one occasion, in the latter part of

* His biographer admits that, upon "sharp affronts he sometimes made sudden returns, and by a word or a *blow* chastised incivilities;" but he harbored no *deliberate* revenge. He possessed eminently a *forgiving spirit.*

his life, he made a splendid entertainment for the ship carpenters of Boston, in the midst of whom he sat down to commemorate God's mercy to him, who had been a ship carpenter himself. And not unfrequently did he affirm, when in the chair of state, that were it not for his obligations to the public, he would much prefer to return to his broad-axe.

In his frequent voyages to and from the eastern parts of Maine, he passed in sight of the hills among which he was born. On such occasions he would call the young soldiers and sailors round him, and speak to them after this fashion: "Young men, it was upon those hills that I kept sheep, only a few years ago. And since you see how the Almighty has led me along, do you learn to fear God, and be honest, and mind your business, and follow no bad courses, and who can tell what he may have in store for you?" And who can tell how much good may have resulted—how many good resolutions may have been awakened and strengthened, in consequence of these homely, but impressive appeals?

Sir William Phipps was an ardent lover of his country; and by his country I mean more especially New England. It will be recollected that, when returning from the West Indies, with his immense cargo of gold and silver, he made a vow, that if the Lord would bring him safe to England, he would forever devote himself to the interests of his people, more especially in the land which gave him birth. This solemn vow was never afterwards forgotten. From that time, he seemed to identify himself with the interests of New England, and to live almost entirely for his country. He was always planning, and laboring, and exposing himself to hardships and perils, for her good. And though he was often ungratefully treated, still his love and his care for her were not diminished. The last thoughts of his busy life were occupied in forming and maturing plans for the welfare of his country.

But the most important trait in the character of Sir William Phipps remains to be mentioned. He was a sincere, devout, and on the whole a consistent Christian. He became deeply impressed with religious truth, under the ministry of Dr. Increase Mather, during the first or second year of his residence in Boston. In subsequent life, he made an open profession of his faith in Christ, and although not free from remaining imperfections, (of which he was himself more sensible than others could be,) yet he adorned that profession to the day of his death. "It was not his habit," says Mather, "to affect any mighty show of devotion; and when he saw persons evidently careful to make a show, who at the same time were defective in the duties of common justice or goodness, he from his heart despised them. Nevertheless, he did show a conscientious desire to observe the laws and ordinances of the Lord Jesus Christ." He was constantly present at the house of God on the Sabbath, and at the stated lectures of the church. He maintained the worship of God, morning and evening, in his family. He usually attended the private religious meetings which devout people observed every fortnight in his neighborhood. When about to undertake any great and difficult enterprise, he would invite some of his Christian brethren to keep a day of fasting and prayer with him at his house. And when success had crowned his undertaking, he would prevail with them to come and keep a day of solemn thanksgiving.

Sir William Phipps was, in the best sense of the term, a *liberal* Christian. He was an earnest advocate of the rights of *conscience*, being equally unwilling to suffer injury himself in this matter, and to injure others. "He did not confine his Christian regards," says Mather, "to this or that sect or party, but wherever he saw the fear and the love of God, whether among Congregationalists, or Presbyterians, or Anti-Pedobaptists, or Episcopalians, he did, without any difference, express towards them a reverent affection."

That he was a man of great personal *courage*, a variety of incidents in his life bear witness; and the foundation of his courage, as he himself explained it, lay in his *piety*. When asked by some one who had observed his valor, what it was that made him so little afraid of dying, his answer was, "I do humbly hope that the Lord Jesus Christ has shed his precious blood for me, and thereby procured my peace with God, and why should I be afraid to die?" A much better answer this—more reasonable, more Christian, than any that should have been based on mere natural fortitude.

The following passage occurs in a sermon preached at Boston, on occasion of the death of Sir William Phipps, by the venerable Dr. Increase Mather; and with it, I close the consideration of his character: "Governor Phipps is now dead, and no longer capable of being flattered; but this I must testify concerning him that though, in the providence of God, I have been much with him, at home and abroad, near at hand and afar off, on the land and on the sea, yet *I never saw him do an evil action, or heard him speak anything unbecoming a Christian.*"

Such then was the man—a puritan, a Christian, a true son of New England, and an ornament of our New England history, whose life and example I have endeavored to portray. I know that my task has been but very imperfectly accomplished. I have said but little, in comparison with what might and ought to be said, in order to a full delineation of the remarkable character which has been before us. But if the facts which have been stated shall have the effect to arouse one of my young readers to greater energy, activity and enterprise, to impress him with sentiments of honor and integrity, to quicken his conscience, to soften his heart, to inspire him with love of country, and the love and the fear of God, and thus lead him on to the possession of a pure, a holy, a spiritual, a useful character;—if such shall be the effect of the memoir, the labor of preparing it will be richly compensated.

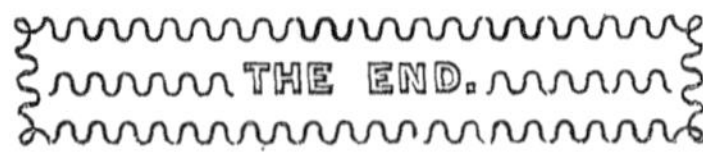

www.ingramcontent.com/pod-product-compliance
Lightning Source LLC
LaVergne TN
LVHW010219110826
845151LV00004B/1142